MW00912401

Someone is Sick in Garfield City

A COLLECTION OF SHORT STORIES

JOEL L. CHINITZ M.D., M.P.H.

More than you ever wanted to know
about our health care system

ISBN: 1-4811-2544-3
ISBN 13: 978-1-4811-2544-4

PREFACE

Someone is Sick in Garfield City is a collection of short stories that consider a range of health care issues in a small, (population 265,310) fictitious south central Pennsylvania City. Despite a common belief, Garfield City was not named for the twentieth U.S. President who, in 1881, was shot by Charles Guiteau, a disappointed, likely schizophrenic (1) office seeker. The city was, in fact, named for Jaspeth Bowling Garfield, a Confederate Army Colonel, whose spleen was nicked twice during a duel at what is now the site of the Mid-Atlantic Medical Center. His was the first of many normal spleens nicked at that site. All the others occurred in operating rooms at the hands of masked men and women with less skill, but more excuses and expletives than Jaspeth Garfield's assailant.

The colonel received a number of other wounds, but, unlike the 20th president, died without the benefit of medical care. The president's demise, on the other hand, likely the consequence of abdominal probing, including a firm poke in the liver by dirty fingers, (2) clearly violated the medical dictum, primum non nocere:

first do no harm. His care, however, did not violate the next dictum, secundum percunium impensa: second, always send a bill despite the outcome. The president's bill, submitted to the Senate, was $85,000 (in 1881 dollars) (3).

Garfield City has two major, and competing, academic medical centers: Garfield University Medical College and Hospital and Mid-Atlantic Medical Center. The following stories, while focusing on events and individuals in these two facilities, consider issues in other venues. Personalities include but are not limited to: Mark Littman, an extremely hard working, dedicated medical resident; Orville Tanchester, a brilliant but psychotic medical student; Jackson Cameron, a department chair, who shared characteristics of both Littman and Tanchester; and Irving Mehlman, whose sample case could change medical education forever. Dave Fisher and Burton Phillips, old-school teachers and clinicians, bear no resemblance to any of the above. The impact of medical technology on health care will be considered, along with the consequences of a) misreading the nametag on a patient's wrist, b) being a target of frivolous lawsuits, c) having your wallet stolen, d) leading the health care industry in patient deaths and e) selling vital body parts.

Someone is Sick in Garfield City is not a standard textbook of medicine. There are no pictures of bloody or bloated organs, no photographs of women with their eyes blocked out while examining their own breasts and no EKGs or MRIs. The word 'prognosis' appears nowhere in the text, neither does 'differential diagnosis', 'broad spectrum antibiotics' or 'idiopathic'. (4) Further, in preparing the volume, no laboratory animals were dropped on their heads to prove the disadvantage of that maneuver on wound healing. Although *Someone is Sick* is intended for informed laymen and consumers, it is written in simple, non-technical language that even physicians can understand.

At the same time, the volume should not be mistaken for a health-care guidebook, and questions such as 'Why do I need hemoglobin A1C' and 'Where are my adrenal glands' will not be addressed. And, with few exceptions, the function of specific body parts is meticulously avoided. That includes the parathyroid glands and the gall bladder. The reader is referred to bookstores where such volumes as *Your Pancreas is Your Friend* and *What is a Gubernaculum and Why* can be found.

Many of the stories, with subsequent revisions, were written between 1989 and 1991 and, unless you are on a low sodium diet, they should be taken with a grain of sodium chloride, a.k.a salt (0.3mg).

Furthermore, while a number of the fictional situations, below, have subsequently occurred, the author denies any responsibility. Truth is often stranger than fiction. (Along with a number of other minor revisions, some of the dates have been changed to conceal the author's age.)

Finally, the author thanks his wife, Joan, for her encouragement and suggestions and for intense editing to bring the manuscript, including spelling and punctuation, to a conventionally acceptable level. Without her input, each story would be a single run-on sentence with no quotation marks or commas.

(1) Not clinically established. (Preceded the DSM)

(2) Sharon Rapp, *Health Letter* 10/12/2012, James Garfield: An assassin's bullet leads to a fate worse than death.

(3) *Useless Information.org.* James Garfield: How Alexander Graham Bell helped to kill the president.

(4) *Ben Clearfield Lady Killer* does, however, include the term 'atelectasis.'

TABLE OF CONTENTS

AND A MAN WHO

"Great news, Senator. Wake-up."

There was no response. The skinny, blue-eyed surgeon, J. Peter Reddington III, leaned over the railing and smiled. He wore a baggy, faded green scrub suit and cracked blood-stained sneakers. A patch of flowered boxer shorts pushed through his torn pants.

"Great news."

Silence. The somnolent patient's mouth hung open, and a column of mucous flowed down the edge of his mouth onto his shoulder. His red eyes circled aimlessly behind dark, swollen lids. He did not move.

"When you were under anesthesia, Senator, we couldn't find that nasty old hernia," Reddington explained. "We explored the area anyway and the inguinal ring was quite strong. Not a bit of protruding tissue, so we were able to close you up quickly."

The lump under the cover kicked and stirred.

"Don't worry. The incision should heal really fast."

The patient drew his arms back and pushed his chest forward. A few moist drops rolled down the surgeon's forehead to his eyebrows.

"Since there wasn't any hernia, Senator Bradfield, I'll charge just half of my usual fee."

Suddenly the bed shook. The patient grabbed the side-rails and pulled himself up.

Reddington stepped back.

"And I'll give you a twenty percent discount on a surgical procedure of your choice for you or any member of your family."

"Hey, I don't know who you are," the lump bellowed. "I don't have no family, and I didn't come here for no hernia. I came in for a sex change operation, man, and you didn't do that either."

The quivering patient, now fully awake, held irrefutable evidence in his right hand and shook it at the glowing surgeon. "You ain't chargin' me a dime, bimbo."

"You're joking, Mr. Bradfield." Reddington pulled his cap off and wiped his forehead. A dark outline of moisture spread across his clinging shirt.

"And I ain't no Bradfield, buddy," the unaltered patient corrected.

""Holy shit!" Reddington screamed as he yanked the patient's hand from the evidence and read the identification bracelet. "RAYMOND BARDFIELD."

The tenured Associate Professor of Surgery, a 1999 Prescott Research Fellow, now mint green, unleashed an assortment of high-pitched primordial incantations and ran from the recovery room with arms swinging wildly. The howling professor charged down a long corridor lined with stretchers and bodies and hurled himself through a set of swinging doors. His right sneaker fell off.

"STOP. Stop the surgery."

Mary Jane Luscowski, operating room supervisor, eternally on guard against chaos in her sterile sanctuary, blocked his path with her outstretched arms. The surgeon, over-matched, bounced off her gloved hands and onto the back wall. Miss Mary Jane, her face revealing neither judgment nor emotion, picked him up and slammed him onto the tile floor.

"STOP. Stop the surgery!" Reddington moaned as she pressed his shoulder against the linoleum. With time, Mary Jane recognizing that P.J. might have a significant matter to discuss, got off his abdomen, lifted him up with her right hand and dusted him off with her left.

"Bardfield. Are you doing a sex job on a guy named Bardfield?" he gasped.

"Room six." The supervisor did not squander words.

"Oooh, no. NO. That's not Bardfield. It's my patient. It's Senator Bradfield."

Reddington limped into Operating Room Six, with Luscowski waddling and huffing behind him. Too late! Two green figures in the corner were tossing wet and bloody towels into a basket. A surgical resident, nestled between a pair of legs, looked up and smiled at the intruders through his mask. He had just finished dressing an area that seemed devoid of its traditional, and highly prized, contents. A red tube poked through the gauze.

"Bardfield?" Reddington asked.

"Right," the intern said, and lifted the patient's wrist in order to demonstrate the nametag. "RAYMOND BRADFIELD."

Reddington's bulging eyes rolled up, his frame became limp, his skin tone faded, and he collapsed onto the operating room floor. Mary Jane and the resident, no longer smiling, dragged him down the hallway and into the locker room.

"Gentlemen, I have a short statement, and then we will take your questions," Lance Walser, Public Relations Director of Garfield University Hospital, announced stiffly. The corner of his left eye twitched. Dr. Benedict Unger, Associate Chairman of the Department of Surgery and Director of the Sexual Ambivalence Correction Service, was standing to his right, carefully studying his shoelaces.

"For more than fifty years," Walser continued, "Garfield University Hospital has combined excellence in teaching, research, and clinical medicine, and today is recognized as one of the leading academic medical centers in the United States." His eyes moved to the back seats. They were empty.

"Our surgical training program is highly regarded. Several former residents now chair departments in prominent medical colleges throughout the country."

The reporters, in various stages of repose and stupor, seemed unmoved. Walser coughed unproductively. His chest expanded and then deflated slowly. The air conditioner hissed and wheezed.

"With this background, I have called today's press conference to announce that this morning, Butch here, uh, Dr. Unger, inadvertently castrated United States Senator Raymond Bradfield."

The reporters, suddenly aroused, jumped up and struggled to understand. What was this man saying? What language was this?

Walser stepped back. His bulging dark eyes darted around the room without settling on a target, and a narrow, rigid smile emerged cautiously below his mustache.

"I am pleased to report," Walser added quickly, "that the surgery was completed in one hour and forty minutes without complications or significant blood loss, and the patient is in the usual stable and satisfactory condition."

The strange words kept coming. The speaker's face became moist and shiny, but his smile held its ground bravely.

"Dr. P.J. Reddington had admitted Senator Bradfield for a left inguinal hernia repair. It is now anticipated that the repair will be performed at a later date…in another institution. I have been advised that Blake Buckley, Director of Citizens for Bradfield, will hold a press conference tomorrow at 9:00 AM to discuss the effects of today's unanticipated event on the senator's campaign for the Democratic Party presidential nomination. Since the senator entered the race as Pennsylvania's favorite son, he may want to revise his strategy. We will now take your questions."

Overhead, the air conditioner died. At the podium, Walser's smile tightened. Although he may have needed the services of a doctor, Unger's shoelaces continued to require his undivided attention.

The cluster of five reporters from the Herald Examiner, the Garfield Daily Record and a few warm and cozy community newspapers could not straighten their tangled thoughts and glared at the men on stage. Rows of dark portraits in the nearly empty auditorium did the same.

The weekly press release had promised only chicken salad and a progress report on the new computerized kitchen and robotic food delivery service. The reporters' mouths hung open. Their heads shook; their eyes froze, and still no questions.

Finally, someone managed to speak. "How on earth could this happen in a totally computerized university hospital with the new Farrington Idiot Proof Identification System?"

"Wasn't the system installed in June after your operating room staff prepped a thirteen year old for a total abdominal hysterectomy?" the Ridgemont Chronicle reporter asked. They all knew that the little darling had been admitted for a rhinoplasty.

"That is correct," Walser replied. His small firm grin did not waver. "In fact, as you meticulously reported, the surgery would certainly have been done had the boy's mother not stubbornly refused permission."

"We have started an investigation of today's incident," Lance continued, "and all the facts will come out. At present we think that the confusion occurred in the pre-op holding area. Because today was a double coupon day, we had the busiest schedule in six months. There were four open hearts, three aortic bypasses, two total colectomies, and a few routine sex changes. The patients were lying side by side, and it may have been a simple matter of an orderly pulling the wrong stretcher into the wrong room or vice versa."

"But isn't a check of the patient's wristband the final step?" Gladys Knowles of the Examiner asked.

"You take that one, Butch," Walser suggested quickly.

Butch looked up. His face suggested that, had he a scalpel, he would gladly have fallen on it. He turned to the blackboard and wrote slowly.

B-R-A-D-F-I-E-L-D   B-A-R-D-F-I-E-L-D

He turned back and folded his arms. The reporters waited for the surgeon to speak, but Butch drew his lips into his mouth, an apparent attempt to swallow them. Twenty-four seconds later, Billy Greene of the Ridgemont Daily Sheet admitted that he didn't get the full meaning of the letters on the board.

"Those are the last names of the patients," Unger indicated with his newfound tongue. "Raymond is the first name of both the senator and the go-go dancer. They both have brown hair and are over 6 feet tall and weigh one hundred and seventy pounds. That is quite a coincidence."

"The senator is fifty three years old. How old is the dancer?" pesky Billy Greene shouted.

"Twenty-two," Unger whispered hoarsely.

"Didn't the patient in your room look older than that?" Gladys Knowles asked.

"No, not really. By the time I entered the surgical suite, the patient was fully prepped and draped. The parts that I saw looked twenty-two." Butch screened his words carefully, spoke slowly, and chose not to mention that the parts were now in the surgical pathology laboratory, if the reporters wished to confirm his clinical impression.

"Didn't the senator's surgeon recognize that the go-go dancer in his OR wasn't his famous patient?"

Unger dropped his chin and covered his mouth with his right hand. If he was sucking his thumb, it was not obvious. Lance Walser, whirling and bouncing, indicated that he would field that question.

"PJ Reddington, the senator's surgeon, was admitted to the hospital today with chest pain and crushed ribs and is unavailable to answer any questions about the attempted hernia repair on the somewhat disgruntled young Mr. Bardfield."

The public relations man's smile widened. "I assume that you will cover this story in tomorrow's edition. Please mention that the dancer will not be charged for this hospitalization."

Hands shot in the air. There was shouting, and the reporters jumped up and down and darted toward the stage. Pads and pencils flew. Walser, back-peddling, thanked them for coming and offered coffee, ballpoint pens and a tour of the new helicopter evacuation pad. Any additional questions regarding today's events would be handled by Dick Englehart of Gladstone, Primrose, West and Henderson. Suddenly, Walser was gone, and Unger dashed after him.

The next morning a crowd filled the Garfield Park Hotel Ballroom and overflowed into the lobby. Senator Raymond H. Bradfield of Pennsylvania, one of twelve candidates for the 2008 Democratic presidential nomination, would have been quite pleased by the turnout of reporters and TV cameras at the press conference, had he not been nursing his ill-placed wound in room 511 of a suddenly famous medical center.

Blake Buckley, the Bradfield Campaign Chairman, raised his arms and called for quiet. The call was unanswered.

"Ladies and gentlemen, you called this the dullest primary campaign since Alton B. Parker led the party to defeat in 1904. You have waited for an issue that would separate the candidates. We are more than pleased to announce that today, in the University Hospital, that issue and that candidate have emerged. Senator and Mrs. Bradfield have…"

"Does the senator plan on remaining in the race?" someone shouted above the clamor.

"Yes, the senator has examined his……eh…...."

"Is he planning on campaigning as a castrato?"

Buckley thrust out his chin and sneered at the questioner.

"Ray Bradfield has discussed his options with his wife, his physicians and the National Council of Women Voters. In eighteen years of public office he has never been neutral on any issue. The senator will complete the surgery and treatments and continue his campaign as a woman."

The rush of questions swelled into a roaring tangle of words and Buckley tried to silence the crowd by screaming answers to unheard or unposed inquiries.

"No, this will not create a constitutional crisis. No, the founding fathers made no provision for this, but the document is quite adaptable, and so is the senator."

"Yes, it is a great opportunity to place a woman in the White House," Buckley shouted. "When the gender change is completed, there will be no other woman in the country with the senator's experience, reputation or wardrobe."

"The transition to complete womanhood will include additional surgery, cosmetics and medications," Buckley concluded.

A group standing on a buffet table shouted that they could not hear Buckley.

"We agree," he continued, "that it is unlikely that a woman could be elected in the next twenty years by any other means."(*)

"No, this was not a planned campaign strategy. Yes, the senator has a reputation for being ambitious, but even he would not have willingly sacrificed his gonads for a stressful low paying four year job."

Suddenly a shrill voice hanging from the balcony rose above the din. "Can the senator really be considered a woman? He has lived as a man for fifty years. Will he truly represent the female perspective?"

The aide explained that, yes, Bradfield would be a perfectly delightful woman. "He has three daughters, two sisters and a female cat and has had extensive exposure to feminine view points. But, obviously, the voters will have to answer that question."

"What about his......what about the senator's relationship to Mrs. Bradfield?"

Buckley thought that, since they had been good friends for many years, they would remain good friends.

"They will live together. There is much that Mildred can teach Ray, and they have already started these discussions. The issue of who will be the first lady and who will be the second one must be resolved, but this will be worked out when the senator is elected."

A chorus of reporters wondered if the senator could focus on the issues following this turn of events.

"No, she will not," Buckley answered proudly. "I challenge you, the press corps, to recall a single campaign in the last thirty years that was not dominated by some sensational disclosure. Candidates have included womanizers, plagiarizers, embezzlers and football players. Issues have never been an issue, nor should they be. It is more important to put someone of character, compassion and integrity in the White House than someone who agrees with you on one or two specifics that will be forgotten between Election Day and the inauguration."

Buckley predicted that his candidate would capture the imagination of the voting public and the cover of every glossy magazine in the world. "Everyone will know his name, and she will win in a landslide. By the way," he concluded, "the name will be Rae Bradfield. The senator is dropping her middle name, Homer."

Two days later and twelve hundred miles away, Boots Presswell walked to the podium and raised his arms. Reluctantly, the modest gathering of reporters, campaign workers and friends stopped drinking, nibbling and chattering.

"Our dream of placing a place-kicker in the White House in 2009 will not be realized," Presswell conceded. That was likely since he received only one percent of the vote in Iowa.

One, perhaps two, bystanders shouted, "No!"

Presswell smiled. "I have reviewed my options and have decided to drop out of the race." He had gotten two percent of the vote in New Hampshire. One bystander shouted, "No!" It may have been the candidate's nephew, Arnold.

Presswell smiled and looked at his misshapen kicking foot. "Throughout history, my friends, major events have been shaped by accidents." Boots looked up. "Wars have been won by accident, fortunes lost by accident and great opportunities created by accident. That is destiny. Rae Bradfield is a candidate who will capture the imagination of the voting public, and I am throwing my support behind the first woman president of this great and glorious land!"

Forty-eight hours later Winslow Thorpe of Maine dropped out of the race in support of the senator from Pennsylvania. "We will be pleased to stand shoulder to shoulder with Rae Bradfield." His campaign manager noted that Thorpe would be equally pleased to have his 27 million dollar campaign debt liquidated.

Within five weeks, as Bradfield was having her hernia repaired, her breasts inserted and hormones injected, Scotty Beisler, John VanderVander and James B. Washington gracefully withdrew from the remaining primaries and asked their supporters to stand behind "the next president of these United States."

Billy Lee Huntshound, on the other hand, remained a dogged and wily campaigner. At the end of May he appeared at an Ohio rally in a long green dress with gold stripes and announced that he too had undergone a sex change. His earrings, which matched his necklace, were a delicate cluster of pearls. He would continue his campaign as the lovely and vivacious Lee Huntshound.

"The country needs a woman president with a southern perspective," he noted in his husky drawl.

Two days before the California primary, however, his claims and his breasts were exposed as a cheap sham. The definitive proof appeared on page 3 of *U.S. Pictorial*, and the former governor of Louisiana dropped out of the race.

As the convention neared, the junior senator from Pennsylvania was the frontrunner. For tall, shapely, deep-voiced Rae Bradfield, adjustment to this new position was a great challenge. Facing screaming crowds was fun. Facing hardboiled reporters was not. Changing locker rooms and partners at the Dexter Tennis Club was easy, walking in three-inch heels was difficult, but, at 6'4", quickly proved unnecessary. Strangely, at every stop the candidate needed to assure the public that she would not get pregnant in the White House.

"Although I have retained my girlish looks, I am fifty one years old." She was actually 53. More importantly, she did not have a uterus, fallopian tubes or any ovaries.

The notorious legislator picked up the women's vote, the Eastern vote, the liberal vote and Dr. Reddington's vote. On July 12, 2008 in Denver, Colorado, Senator Rae Bradfield won the Democratic Party nomination on the first ballot.

Four months later, Rae Bradfield, presidential in a red suit and white blouse with a fluffy collar, waved to acknowledge the cheers of the crowd. The large campaign button, 'IT'S TIME FOR A

CHANGE'; was still on her lapel; and her friend, Mildred, was at her side. She had just been elected president by the largest plurality in 56 years.

"This is a great day for women and a great day for America," the president-elect shouted.

It wasn't a great day for Butch Unger. None had been lately. Although Bradfield had won in a landslide, it was unlikely that Dr. Unger would be the next Secretary of Health. The best he could hope for was to be the answer to the most popular trivia question in the history of the civilized world.

"Fate and Garfield University Hospital have given me a great opportunity," Bradfield continued, "and I will take full advantage of that. Last year I was an obscure candidate. In January I will be your president." The cheers erupted again.

"I will take that opportunity to bring a new perspective to the old office. I will take this opportunity to examine the effects that two hundred years of male domination have had on the executive branch of government."

It was hard to remember that the president-elect had been a man for fifty-three years and a woman for eight months.

"For too many years, policy in this country has been based on machismo," she continued. "Compassion has been mistaken for weakness. As a result we have drifted into a world of football clichés and beer commercials. Drifting, while many among us are out of work and homeless, while many of us cannot get health care(**) and where some see greed as the only virtue."

"Drifting," she emphasized, "in an increasingly dangerous and violent world in which we cannot define our objectives, while a growing number of nations have nuclear weapons and terrorism dominates the global picture."

Some of the guests wondered if this was the same person who had announced his candidacy in a Garfield Eagles' football jersey, while sitting in front of his gun collection.

"I now call for a new era in the chief executive's office. I call for a re-evaluation of our policies and institutions. Next week I will release the names of my cabinet appointees. The list will include some of our most qualified women. The list will include other segments of our diverse population that have been under-represented for two hundred years." Bradfield waved to the crowd and stepped back while adjusting her slip.

Shouts of "Rae, Rae" filled the room. As Mildred and Rae left the ballroom, the clamor continued. Outside, surrounded by secret service agents and the still immovable Mary Jane Luscowski, they stopped to answer questions.

"Would the president resign from the all male Provost Club?"

Bradfield smiled. No answer.

"What would the president wear to the inaugural ball? Whom would she dance with?"

Bradfield smiled.

"Does the president-elect still smoke cigars?"

Bradfield smiled again and turned toward her car.

"What was the president's first priority?"

Bradfield, no longer smiling, turned back.

"There is much to be done," she noted. "Where do we start? Well.....the medical community ripped me apart and had to rebuild me. I think it resulted in a better product. Now it's medicine's turn for radical surgery." Her eyes gleamed. "We'll start there. See you in January."

With skillful manipulation of her abdominal wall, Mary Jane cleared a path, and the first and second ladies slipped into their limousine and were gone. The staff of the prestigious Garfield University Hospital knew that they would be back.

(*) This account, necessitating a gender change, preceded the current political climate where it will not take surgery or twenty years to elect a woman.

(**) This account preceded the Affordable Health Care Act.

THE GONE-A-GRAM

"Have I got this right? When you …eh….reach eighty points…. you're gone."

"Yes, sir. That's right."

"But if you have seventy nine….you're still here."

Harry Crenshaw looked into the faces around the conference table. Why didn't the hospital research committee take his project seriously? The study was valid and clinically applicable. Maybe Janine was right; he should not have called it "The Gone-A-Gram."

"Your statistics, the numbers, seem fine, son, but you might have trouble with public acceptance," old Doc Scattergood warned, benignly shaking a gnarled and speckled finger at Crenshaw.

"Will a man understand if you tell him that dear old Uncle Mortimer is going to die because he has eighty-three points, just three over the limit? It certainly is a pity to kill someone for a few lousy points."

"Sir, we don't actually kill anyone," Crenshaw protested hoarsely. "We just stop taking care of them."

With that, Charlie Scattergood, who had been around since the days that a surgeon could go to church and take out an appendix in the same suit, twisted in his chair. Although not truly somber looking, he was no longer smiling.

"Stop taking care of patients, you say?" Scattergood, pulling on his right ear, thought that his hearing was not what it once was.

Lance Needleman, representing the Department of Surgery, threw down the battered remnant of a salami sandwich that had survived three earlier interviews and a trip to the bathroom. "So you use your computer to terminate care," Needleman shouted, in a tone usually reserved for overworked, sleep-deprived interns with the temerity to pass out on his operative field and not for a research fellow who was presenting the findings of a three-year study.

"No, that's not what I mean," Crenshaw stammered. "We just use the Gone-A-Gram as an objective indicator of the patient's chances of recovery. When patients reach eighty points, they cannot survive. The mortality rate is one hundred percent." Harry seemed anxious to make that his concluding statement.

Most of the committee seemed equally anxious, but Burt Phillips, the Director of Nephrology, had one final question. "Do you ever have double coupon days?" Phillips asked.

Crenshaw squinted without answering, clearly unprepared for the question. Undoubtedly, he had not considered any introductory offers.

"I mean, do you ever have discount days, one cent sales or bonus points?" Phillips asked. "Buy one, get one free?"

"No, sir. We don't use gimmicks." Crenshaw was sweating freely. "It's simple. We just add up the points. One point for every antibiotic after the first two. Those are free." His collar was now darker than the rest of this shirt, and his tie was a bit spongy.

"Add six points for every week on a respirator and five if your blood pressure is below eighty for seventy two hours. The chart on page twelve lists what you get if your pupils are unequal, if you vomit blood or if one of your big toes falls off. When you have more than four I.V. lines, you ....."

"That's fine, Harry," Dr. Hastings, the committee chair, interrupted. "We have the full list. That part is quite clear, but since you do not terminate care at eighty points, what is the purpose of your system?"

Crenshaw filled his lungs quickly and explained, as he wrung out his tie on the report, that it was a guide to assist families in making decisions about further high tech studies and other life saving treatments such as baboon heart pumps and pig liver perfusion. "If the patient has more than eighty points, we would tell the family not to do it."

"And, of course, the families listen to that advice."

"No, sir, that is one problem with the Gone-A-Gram," Crenshaw responded flatly, wiping his face with pages forty-seven and forty eight of the report. "The families never listen."

"Why do you suppose that is?" Hasting wondered.

"I can't say for sure, but perhaps at those critical times they react emotionally rather than logically." The committee appeared ready to accept that premise. "But," Crenshaw continued, "sometimes the families have motives that we don't know about."

No one on the committee knew what that meant.

"Well, eh, turn to page one hundred thirty seven, for example: the case of Arnold T. Sylvester. He was admitted last August with a massive stroke. His blood pressure was high, his blood count was low and his kidneys shut down when he had eighty nine points."

The men around the table opened their red covered booklets. Scattergood's copy was upside down.

"We told his wife that he would die if he didn't have dialysis, but we didn't recommend it because he had too many points. Mrs. Sylvester said, 'Do it anyway.' "

"Didn't you explain that according to the computer, her husband had no chance of recovery?" Hastings asked.

"We did, but she said, 'Do it anyway.' So we did it. We had to. Then a week later a social worker told me that Mr. Sylvester gets a monthly disability check. If he was dead, he would no longer be considered disabled, and his wife wouldn't get the five hundred and forty seven dollar payment. Mrs. Sylvester and his sister Irene need the money. If they can't come up with another sickly relative when Arnold dies, one of them will have to find an outside job."

"You don't mean that he's still alive?"

"Yes, sir, he's alive…well, sort-of. He's all curled up, and we can't uncurl him anymore. He has a feeding tube, a trach and a pacemaker, and we had to sew his eyes shut to keep them in their sockets." Harry puffed out his chest. "Now he has four hundred seventy seven points."

Orville Hastings rolled up the report and tossed it on the table while turning toward his colleagues for further questions or comments. Charlie Scattergood closed his eyes and shook his head. Skinny Darwin McAllister, the newest member, put his feet under his rump and drew himself up into a ball. Darwin wasn't a clinician, and he clearly had no questions about this kind of stuff.

"Thank you, Harry. Please go. I mean, eh, you are free to go," Hastings said. "We will announce the winner of the Louis Pasteur-Walter Reed award in ten days."

As Harry, head down, slithered out, the research committee members, having completed all the interviews, scratched, stretched, yawned and redistributed themselves among the reports of the young investigators. Scattergood, on the other hand, while seemingly alive, was rigid.

Lance Needleman loosened his tie, tossed a chunk of salami from his lap and announced the Gone-A-Gram was an incredibly sloppy piece of work. "I'm voting for Terry Robinson's nuclear powered, implantable gall bladder. It's a great engineering concept."

"Yeah, what an incredible breakthrough," Phillips rebutted. "Can't you see the hordes lining up to have radioactive pumps shoved under their livers so that they can digest pepperoni pizza?"

"Well," Needleman huffed, drawing his chin back, "it may not fill an immediate need, but it is a prototype for other replacement parts. The graphite rod plutonium sphere could be an excellent source of energy for a range of mechanical replacement parts."

"Great, just great," Phillips sneered. "Now a doctor will never know when a water-cooled patient might walk into his office, blow up in his face and level the city."

Darwin McAllister, shaking, pushed his chair back from the table, dropped his head between his knees and drew his legs up to his chest.

"Burt's right," Hastings added, patting McAllister on his head. "We need safe, practical projects like David Tressler's density-mass study. The technology is already in place, and there will be no melt-down or radioactive turds."

"What's more, it's YOUR technology." Phillips whirled in his chair to face Hastings. "And Tressler is over his head. What does he know about radionuclide physics? He doesn't even know which end of the stethoscope to put in his ears."

"He doesn't have a stethoscope," Hastings protested. "But we've had some of the equipment for two years and have done fifty atomic absorption studies to determine average body density.

That's simple. When we install the new magnetic scanner, we will program it for total body volume."

Phillips, looking over the figures, wondered why anyone would need precise body density and volume measurements.

"That's just the point," Hastings added quickly, banging his fist on the table. "When you multiple the volume and the density you get the patient's total body mass."

Phillips had heard enough. "Total body mass? You can get the same results by stepping on a damn bathroom scale."

"If you want to look at it that way, I guess you could," Hastings acknowledged, clutching the table. "You could use a scale if you wanted to stop medical progress, but no one weighs patients anymore. And furthermore," he continued, giving Phillips his best conspiratorial wink, "we can bill twelve hundred bucks for each study."

"Yeah, I agree." McAllister, Director of the Genetics Laboratory, stopped rocking, unfurled slowly and looked up. "We must never stand in the way of imaginative, profitable technology. But that's why I favor Bergman's project," McAllister squeaked. "Imagine, programming rhesus monkeys to do vascular surgery. Brilliant."

With that, Needleman stopped peeling his banana and shoved it in the pocket of his bloody lab coat. "It'll never work."

"Why not?" McAllister asked. "Have you ever watched monkeys pick fleas out of their buddies' ears? They have great small motor coordination. Bergman just inserts a computer chip in their right frontal lobe and programs it to direct those muscles appropriately. He is almost ready for a clinical trial."

Needleman, who had, indeed, watched a few monkeys during his surgical training, suggested that McAllister might want to volunteer to be the first to have his aorta bypassed by a programmed hairy ape.

That woke Scattergood. "How will a person react when he meets his surgeon and he's bouncing up and down scratching his belly?"

"That happens all the time," Hastings snickered. "And the families almost never meet the surgeons. No one has to know."

"Right," McAllister chirped. "We can hide the cages and put human names on the bills. When you think about it, the thing really does make sense."

Burt Phillips pressed the heels of his hands into his eyes, leaned forward and did think about it. Smiling to himself, he wondered what would happen if the computer chip slipped and the monkey could only do orthopedic surgery? No longer smiling he thought about some of the older projects – more potent diuretics – newer antibiotics – pacemakers and defibrillators. That was the golden age of medicine: new technology was our servant. Now is it our master?"

"Come on, fellas, time marches on," Hastings announced. "As Hippocrates said, we cannot stand in the way of progress. Time to vote."

24 PLASTIC CADAVERS WITH HEAVY-DUTY HINGES

"No, Senator, the brightest students become the brightest doctors, not the best doctors. That requires hard work, understanding, attention to detail and love."

Burton Phillips M.D., F.A.C.P.
Professor of Medicine
Mid-Atlantic College of Medicine
In testimony before the Senate Select Committee
investigating the inadvertent castration of
President-elect Bradfield.

"Mr. Mehlman, eh, Dr. Mehlman. Stop!"

Irving Mehlman lowered his head and kept walking. He gripped his sample case with both hands and swung it as he marched down the hallway, alternately lurching forward and swaying back. A guy in a white jacket with stuffed pockets ran after him, waving his arms, shouting and jumping in the air. The jumper, younger, taller, trimmer and unencumbered by a sample case, caught up with Mehlman before he reached the stairway.

"Don't you recognize me?" the young man asked, wheezing, as he slid in front of Mehlman and extended his arms. "Littman. I'm Mark Littman."

Searching for a path around the obstacle, Mehlman turned sharply, flinging his case to the left. His shoulders dropped, and the clump of hair intended to cover his scalp swung over his eyes and nose.

"Don't you remember me from St. Bruce?" Littman pleaded, shifting to the left. "I went to your medical school."

"No. No, I don't remember you," Mehlman shouted as he pivoted toward the main lobby and dashed away. "Gotta go."

Littman caught up with him in front of the gift shop. "I was a resident at Maxwell after I graduated," he explained. Littman was gulping air. "And I was off-shore graduate of the year."

"That's swell, kid. See ya later." As Littman was deflating, Mehman dropped his case and took off again. Littman picked it up and ran after him.

"How are things at St. Brucey's? Do you still teach biochem in the fertilizer warehouse?" Littman screamed down the hallway, still breathless.

"Exploded and burned to the ground."

People in the corridor backed away to clear a path for the runners.

"Do you still have those shiny plastic cadavers with removable blood vessels?"

"In storage."

"Oh." The smile on Littman's face fell. "Why are you here? Why aren't you on the island?"

"I'm meeting with the dean," Mehlman shouted over his shoulder.

"We don't have one," someone in the audience yelled.

"I mean the assistant dean. That's right, I'm meeting with.... with... eh." His eyes rolled up. "Cal Geckler." The veins in Mehlman's neck bulged, and his head, starting at the collar line, was turning purple.

"I don't know him," Littman replied. His arms were wrapped around the sample case. "Are you going to affiliate here? That's great."

They reached a corner, and both men stopped abruptly. As Littman fell forward, Mehlman put his hands up to keep the case from impaling him against the molding. The case pressed against his rib cage, and he shifted his hips to get free; but Littman was draped over him, and his wiggling wedged them into a corner. Mehlman's nostrils flared, and his head and eyes, like a sparrow's, darted around for an opening.

"You sent me to a skin hospital in Idaho for all of my clinical rotations," Littman continued, sighing between words. "It was terrible. Why don't you affiliate here with Mid-Atlantic?"

"I can't do it," Mehlman moaned, throwing his head back to get the hair off his face. "Look, kid, we went under."

"Went under?" Littman repeated and pulled back.

"Bankrupt. Folded."

The crowd that had gathered around them sighed.

''I sold what I could at auction," Mehlman explained.

Littman tightened his jaw and looked down at his feet. "Gee, that won't look so good on my staff applications." In tears, he handed the case back.

"Hung in long as I could, but competition from the damn mainland schools got too much. They all increased class size to make ends meet."

Littman looked up and shook his head. Most of the crowd did the same.

"And now nobody wants to be a doctor." Mehlman took a handkerchief from his jacket pocket and wiped his forehead. Then, with a thin smile, he wished everyone well, cleared a path with his sample case and bolted up the hallway and down the stairs. Littman would have to find his own way of telling his friends and future employers that his medical school was liquidated in a going-out-of-business sale.

At the foot of the stairs, Mehlman followed the signs to 'Receiving'. The supply office door was open at the top and torn from the frame at the bottom. Inside, a dozen snoring bodies on folding chairs slumped on either side of a secretary. A few were covered with dust and bits of debris. One was curled up on the floor, face down, snoring.

Irving Mehlman walked up to the desk and dropped his case. Nothing. He picked it up and dropped it again. "Kindly tell Mr. Geckler that Dr. Mehlman is here to see him."

Except for the jaw, the secretary's head, hovering over a magazine, did not move.

"I think that Mr. Geckler will want to see me as soon as possible, madame," Mehlman shouted. He tried to get his pinky ring to shine in her eyes, but there wasn't enough light.

"The gentleman can take a number and have a seat or come back tomorrow," Sylvia, the secretary said, pushing a wad of food into the corner of her mouth with her tongue.

Mehlman yanked a red seventeen from a hook hanging over a rusty file cabinet. "Is it always this crowded?" he asked.

"The gentleman can wait near the water cooler with other salesmen or come back tomorrow," the woman said flatly, keeping her head down.

Mehlman unfolded a plastic chair that was leaning against a cardboard carton and sat next to a man in red pants and a green corduroy jacket. He was wearing a bolo tie. His legs were crossed, a newspaper was folded on his lap, his eyes were closed, and he rested his chin on his hand.

"She always wants us to come back tomorrow. Tomorrow they're closed," the man muttered without opening his eyes or mouth.

Mehlman took the man's newspaper and fanned himself.

"Number eight," the women called out.

Eight. Was this the way to treat seventeen, the founder and sole owner of an accredited medical school? Fully licensed by the Imperial Government of Grand Saint Bruce Island? No. Mehlman stood, ripped seventeen to shreds, dropped the newspaper and his chair into a trash bin, stepped over the man on the floor and leaned across the secretary's desk. Lifting her round face from the magazine, she yawned.

"Are you eight?"

"No," Mehlman answered. "I'm 'friggin' seventeen."

"Well, seventeen, you are casting a shadow across my magazine. The gentleman can..........."

"Madame, kindly tell Mr. Geckler that DOCTOR Mehlman is STILL here to see him," he interrupted. "I don't think you get too many doctors down here."

She closed her magazine and tossed it on her pasta salad. She had to admit that very few doctors wander down to the loading ramp. She did not need to know that Mehlman's doctorate was an honorary degree from the Grand St. Bruce College of Floral Design.

"Furthermore, young lady, I attended this medical school while you were still in diapers."

The secretary tucked a few loose strands of hair back into place and smiled, exposing bits of vegetables in spaces once occupied by teeth.

"Class of '84, darling," Mehlman explained without adding that he was kicked out in '81.

Although his mother wanted him to be a rich and famous physician, and although he slept with his head on the eighty-fifth edition of <u>Gray's Anatomy</u>, he could never remember the difference between the pre-frontal lobes and the fifth cranial nerve. And the instructors seemed to dwell on those details. Somewhere between freshman orientation and the eight essential amino acids, or was it ten, the Professors of Anatomy, Biochemistry and Physiology concluded that young Irving, despite his sincerity and charm, was better suited for a different career. Perhaps stock options and land speculation.

"Perhaps the doctor came to the wrong office?"

"No, sweetheart. I don't actually practice medicine. Right now I have a great line of talking stethoscopes that the sophomore class will fall in love with. And who wouldn't? They come in five colors."

He handed her a glossy brochure and a business card with the address of the <u>I.T.M. Medical Education Supply Company</u>. Then Mehlman handed a card to a man standing behind him who claimed to be number eight. In the center the words "Meeting the needs of tomorrow's famous doctors" circled a pair of pink dancing bandage scissors.

"I can let Geckler have twelve on consignment."

As Mehlman was explaining the computer features of his equipment to number eight, a red light on a box next to the secretary's telephone flashed, and a booming voice filled the room, waking the man on the floor.

"Sylvia, get the hell in here right away!"

Sylvia picked up her pasta salad and ran in. When she waddled back out, the voice was right behind her. It belonged to Geckler, and he was leaping over bodies and heading out the door. Number eight stepped back, and Mehlman picked up his display case and ran. He caught up with Geckler in time to squeeze into an elevator as the doors were closing.

Mehlman smiled.

"What the hell do you want? Aren't you the guy I kicked out last week?"

Mehlman thought that it might have been a guy who looked like him. "I have a full line of educational supplies, new and used; and a special tutorial program for shy and less gifted sophomores. Perhaps Mr. Geckler would like to see my pharmacology building blocks. Perhaps I can interest you in designer ophthalmoscopes. Rechargeable batteries."

"You are the guy," Geckler shouted.

"Or maybe you prefer pre-inflated blood pressure cuffs?" Mehlman replied, as he backed into a corner. "In a turquoise velveteen case."

"No." Geckler preferred that Mehlman get lost. "Our school has a major crisis. If you can't come up with thirty-four cadavers by Monday, would you please get out of my way?"

"Would twenty-five help?" Mehlman asked as they reached the fourteenth floor, and Geckler, head down, marched toward two large walnut doors.

"I might have twenty-eight," Mehlman corrected, as he slid into the office behind Geckler.

"You can go right in, Cal. The president is waiting for you," a young women said as she pointed her emery board toward another set of heavy doors.

The president, T. Graton Stiffleigh, was pacing back and forth in front of his desk, rubbing his hands. Occasionally, he looked up toward the ceiling. Occasionally, he kicked a golf ball. He wore a red and blue school tie, and his sleeves were rolled up so that a set of cuff links dangled near his elbows.

Geckler coughed, and Stiffleigh stopped marching.

"What's that behind you?" Stiffleigh asked. Geckler turned around as Mehlman ducked behind a rubber tree. He turned sideways, but his exposed diameter was unchanged.

"Damn it, Cal. This really looks bad," the president sputtered. "We're not going to get any of our bodies back. Someone just tossed a note through my window."

"All the way to the fourteenth floor?" Mehlman whispered and sucked in his belly. He was still too big for the tree.

Stiffleigh pointed to a brick on the credenza. "It came with a note from the Garfield City Death with Dignity Committee. They claim to be the group that broke into the anatomy lab and stole all the cadavers. The "Death" chairman said that they held a delightful service that 'spoke to the dignity of the human body' and then buried the corpses on a lovely dairy farm in Stibbleworth, West Virginia."

"I wish I could have been there," Mehlman said. Geckler reached around the tree, grabbed Mehlman's collar and pulled him toward the door.

Stiffleigh sat down on his desk. "We're ruined. Ruined."

"How about the Brompton Street Cadaver Clearing House?" Geckler asked, still clutching Mehlman's collar. "They must have a few left."

"They have seven in usable condition, but Death with Dignity is picketing their warehouse."

"Can't we use another supplier?" Geckler asked. He had a firm grip on Mehlman's jacket with Mehlman slung over his shoulder.

"Brompton Street is the only cadaver retailer east of the Mississippi."

"Why don't we start the year without them?" Geckler asked. Mehlman's feet were dangling a foot and a half above the carpet.

"Nope. Can't do that. Bad for our image," Stiffleigh explained. "When the public thinks about medical education, what do they think of?"

"CADAVERS!" Mehlman shouted over Geckler's shoulder.

"That's right, Calvin," Stiffleigh responded. "Garfield University was tipped off and has armed guards in the anatomy lab around the clock. They repulsed two invasions, wounded a sniper and lost only one body. And they have cadavers upstate. We're ruined." A tear welled up in the corner of his right eye and trickled down his cheek.

"Know just how you feel, buddy. We had the same problem at my place," Mehlman replied sympathetically as he swung his leg around and kicked Geckler on the knee.

Stiffleigh rubbed his eyes and looked down. "Who, may I ask, are you?"

"Hey, just get outta here and leave us alone," Geckler demanded as he reached for the salesman's arm.

"Wait a minute, Cal. You had the same problem?" the president asked. "What do you mean?"

"I had an image problem at my medical school, too," Mehlman explained. "Because it's hot and muggy, they cremate everyone on St. Bruce Island. There are tough laws against dead people. I couldn't get any cadavers, so, finally, I made my own."

The president wanted to hear more.

"And they are beautiful," Mehlman explained. He stood up, pulled a shiny brochure out of his case and pointed to pictures of two full-sized, vinyl coated plastic bodies with heavy-duty hinges. "They come in male and female."

Stiffleigh, having gotten an A in sex education at Bartholomew Prep, knew that.

"I can let you have the males for twelve hundred bucks apiece. The females are fifty dollars more," the salesman explained as he pulled out his order book.

"But the female is smaller," Geckler protested.

"Shut up, Cal. Money is not the issue. We are fighting for survival. We'll take thirty-four and a half."

"…..fraid I can't break up a unit."

Stiffleigh understood. They would take thirty-five.

Mehlman had only twenty-seven, maybe twenty-eight. Could they start with that?

Of course they could.

"Can I fix you up with anything else today, gentlemen? Maybe a nice DVD of enzymatic digestion in the jejunum? In color. The guy who plays bile juice could win an Oscar."

"Maybe some other time, Mr……eh."

"Perhaps an accounts receivable manual for the seniors. Very popular across town at snooty Garfield Medical School."

"Nothing else, thank you, unless you have a dean and vice-president of academic affairs in your sample case," Stiffleigh added. "The Committee for Safe and Sane Medical Education burned his office down, and the dean fled to Cape Cod."

"It's nice there at the end of the season. And the Vice-President for Academic Affairs?" Mehlman asked.

"It's the same guy."

"And he left because of one lousy fire. I've had four or five." Mehlman pursed his lips and shook his head. "Nothing showy. Just nice little fires."

"It's not just the fire. The last two or three years have not gone well for Mid-Atlantic," Stiffleigh explained as he watched Mehlman pull a sliver of glass from his pants. "Garfield Trust put a lien on our electron microscope. We've got only one research grant, for a non-toxic nail polish. We are forty-four million dollars in debt, and we all took a pay cut. The dean was about to leave anyway."

"Know just what you mean. The medical school business isn't what it used to be. Too much overhead, too many regulations and too much competition."

"And applications are falling off. We didn't fill the freshman class this year," Stifleigh said and sat on his desk.

Mehlman dropped his case, walked around the mahogany desk, plopped into the leather swivel chair and settled his elbows on the blotter. He fingered a gold pen. "Did you try selling the school?"

"No." Stiffleigh did not think he could find a buyer. "Was Mr.......eh.... interested?"

"No, thanks," Mehlman responded quickly, "but maybe I can help you with a nice little fire?" He pulled out several pictures of burning buildings from his sample case and spread them across the blotter.

Stiffleigh squinted and shook his head. He appreciated the offer and thought that fire number three was perfect, with clean lines and the right blend of earth tones and sparkling colors. But he had to decline. "I hope that you understand. I have to answer to the Board of Directors, and they tend to be rather traditional."

Mehlman understood and, by the way, Mr. President, for the cadavers, naturally, it's C.O.D.

"Come in, Mr. Mehlman. I'm glad you could make it." President Stiffleigh stood and motioned for his guest to sit.

"Hey, my pleasure, Graton. Is there anything I can do for you?" Mehlman took the cigar from his mouth, and they watched the ashes fall onto the rug.

"The freshmen are here. The kids are getting restless, and I had hoped that we would be getting some of the cadavers by Tuesday. That's when tuition is due."

"Didn't Geckler tell you? I delivered twelve last week, ten male, two female, but Cal didn't have the cash. He handed me a purchase order."

Stiffleigh pushed his chair back and closed his eyes.

"I can accept a purchase order from a plumber or a department store, not from a medical school. You understand what I'm telling you?"

Stiffleigh understood. But he simply did not have enough funds to pay for the bodies. They sold nine gallons of the non-toxic nail polish, but the bank took the receipts, and the school has no other liquid assets.

Mehlman dropped his cigar in the Bromley Yacht Club ashtray and pushed the chair back. "You need cash, sonny, so you'd better take some advice. You're running this shop like it was 1980. Well, times have changed."

That might be true, but President Stiffleigh did not want a fire.

"I'm not talking about that," Mehlman scolded. "I looked around the place. You have three lecture halls that seat two hundred. How large is each class?"

"Two twenty. We had to expand."

"Right," Mehlman continued, "not enough room if everyone went to class. But how many students go to the lectures?"

Stiffleigh didn't know. He used to have a dean who could answer that question. He had more important things and the board to worry about.

"For a good lecture, maybe eleven," Mehlman answered. "For Professor Clyde Rustin in microbiology, the note taker shows up, turns on his tape recorder and walks out."

What could Stiffleigh do about it? He couldn't afford anyone better than Rustin.

"Then close those big rooms. You're throwing away a fortune in heat and electricity. Or turn it into a bowling alley. That'll get the students back into the building where they'll spend some money in the cafeteria."

Stiffleigh wondered how the students were learning if they didn't come to lectures.

"From the computer programs and DVDs you supply. And you let the kids use them free. Even at just ninety-nine cents a night, the DVDs would pay for the cadavers in three months."

Mehlman stood, walked over to Stiffleigh and patted him on the shoulder. "Merchandising, my friend. Times change, and you have got to change with them."

Stiffleigh thought that he had been happier in his father-in-law's sporting goods business.

"And as far as your enrollment problem is concerned," Mehlman advised, "open your doors a little wider. The bright ones are going into wealth management and computers, so take the students who aren't as bright."

The president reminded him that there were regulations that could not be broken.

"So pull and bend them a little," Mehlman suggested. "You can run your own admissions preparation course. Teach a little biology and some calculus and physics. I can sell you some organic chemistry coloring books."

Stiffleigh, eyes wide, wondered how low he could stoop.

"That, my friend, is strictly up to you, but I can help."

The president smiled. "Thank you, Irving. How can I ever repay you for this?"

"Hello……..I am calling with a very brief message."

"Lionel, who is on the phone?"

"It's one of those damn computer messages."

"Allow me to introduce myself. My name is DOCTOR Irving T. Mehlman. I am calling from the Mid-Atlantic College of Medicine."

"Why don't you hang up?"

"Wait a minute, Joyce. It's a doctor."

"I am the Vice-president and Most Senior Dean of the College, and I am calling to tell you that a quality medical education is within your reach."

"He says that I can become a doctor."

"Sure, Lionel, tell that to the guys in the shop. They may want to join you."

"At Mid-Atlantic we have brought the exciting and rewarding career of medicine within the reach of every citizen. If you can read your newspaper without help, you will have no trouble meeting the admission requirements of this fully accredited school."

"Hang up! I'm waiting for a call from Grace."

"Shhh."

"…….easy to reach by public transportation, and there is ample parking for your car or truck. In addition, we have many payment plans, and loans are available to qualified applicants. Do not let money stand in the way of fulfilling your lifelong dream or your mother's dream."

"Give me that phone, you idiot."

"Feel insecure? Afraid to take a chance? There is no need to give up your current job to attend. Part-time, evening, week-end, study at home and patient simulation programs are available at truly affordable rates."

"You could never get your hands clean enough to become a doctor. Look at that phone. Give it to me."

"Not for me. I was thinking that maybe Jimmy next door might want to go."

"Jimmy? The nose-picker? He just flunked out of Maxwell Photography School."

"So what. I see him reading the paper all the time. He reads good."

"..........and for your dining pleasure while training, Mid-Atlantic has several fine restaurants and the famous Sir William Osler cocktail lounge. Bowling too, my friends. Just call 1-800-BE-AN-MD2. Operators are standing by to take your call."

"I'm going to kill you," Joyce shouted.

Lionel burped and hung up.

IT'S A COMPLEX WORLD

Author's note: This account includes a medical student's critique of how the volume of our body fluid is estimated. Rather than directly measuring the actual volume, we use the pressure in our small arteries as a gauge of total body water. When that pressure is low, the fluid volume is considered low. This can underestimate the actual volume when the heart is pumping weakly (heart failure), and this causes us to retain salt and water, which makes the heart failure even worse.

The maintenance of precise body fluid volumes is vital to all mammals including people. Why then did nature equip us with a totally worthless method of measuring and adjusting that volume? Our volume sensors have caused more problems than all the wars in recorded history (So far).

Pg. 3 <u>My Computer Model for Correcting Major Flaws in Human Design.</u> Senior Paper – Elville M. Tanchester, 4th Year Class, Mid-Atlantic College of Medicine, Garfield City, Pennsylvania

"Yes, it is an incredibly complicated world, young man; a tangle of time and space, mass and energy."

Dean Morris Rhodeway leaned forward. A hint of color spread across his clay cheeks, and his eyes, no longer stuck midway between indifferent and dead, widened. Across his desk, the young man in a once white lab coat, Elville Morrison Tanchester, half swallowed by a malevolent chair, pushed back in an effort to preserve a remnant of the safety zone normally accorded political prisoners.

"I believe that there are limits to human comprehension; things that we were never meant to understand. If nothing else, Mister Tanchester, you have proven that."

Tanchester, a Mid-Atlantic Medical College senior, felt heat rise from his neck and settle on the tips of his long sensitive ears. He tightened his jaw. Tanchester's academic record, scattered across the dean's desk, was testimony to his unique cerebral pathways. Why then did he have to defend himself against the charges of an incompetent faculty?

"I can understand your desire to simplify cardiac physiology, if that was your intent," the dean continued, emphasizing every word, "but your ideas are…..they are CRAZY!"

That was too much emphasizing for Tanchester. He preferred the dean's usual torpor to this diatribe.

"You don't understand. I was merely trying to explain why Man develops heart failure so frequently," he rebutted.

"Perhaps. Perhaps in your way you have," Rhodeway conceded, "but was it necessary to say that the entire human excretory and circulatory systems are defective because of criminal wrong doing during the mammalian planning and construction phases?"

Now Tanchester had him. "I am not afraid of the truth," he shouted. "I have irrefutable evidence that the human heart and blood vessels were designed by scoundrels and political appointees and assembled by a gang of idiots."

"Who gave you the assignment of analyzing creation?" The dean pulled the pipe out of his mouth and banged it on Tanchester's manuscript. "The senior paper should be a well-documented presentation of the causes, manifestations and management of a single disease. Any disease, but it has got to be a real one."

Apparently the dean was shifting the emphasis of this trial to divert responsibility. The student, now sweating, sank further into the chair.

"What does this statement mean?" Rhodeway picked up the soiled report. "Lazy, misguided mammals borrowed equipment from worms and other primitive forms of life."

The heat was oppressive. Tanchester started to unbutton his soggy shirt. "Obviously I mean that we should have built our own high-tech devices."

"That's not how things work around here. Are you opposed to evolution?" the dean shouted.

"No, it had its place, but why did we copy sensing devices from spineless little slime without hearts? They work fine for those creatures, but not for us." He took his lab coat off, curled it up and tossed it on the floor. "In heart failure those cheap sensors misfire."

Tanchester stood and banged his fist on the desk. "Because those sensors give false information, we tighten our blood vessels, and that makes it even harder for the heart to pump."

"That may be true," the dean stammered, "but what can we do about it? It's a little late to change human development to retrofit your new equipment."

"I know that," Tanchester shot back. "Do you think I'm crazy?"

Rhodeway pulled his head back and squinted. Tanchester had seen that look before.

"You recommended that we convene a congressional committee to investigate your charges of faulty equipment, corruption
and bodily mismanagement. Well, we are certainly not going to
do that."

That did not surprise Tanchester.

"Frankly, I am more concerned about the equipment between
your ears. In thirty-four years I've never seen a medical student
like you. Look at yourself. Your shoes don't match, and you're
wearing two ties."

Elville had not remembered putting either tie on. He sat down
and tried to pull off the green one. The dean, still looking rather
upset, made no effort to help.

"If you insist, I'll rewrite the paper," Tanchester conceded. He
could play their silly game. He had done it before. "I can leave out
the good parts that upset you."

"No, I don't want you to revise it, and stop fussing with your
clothes. I am recommending to the discipline and promotions
committees that you not graduate with your class."

"Fine!" Tanchester wanted to know when he would graduate.
He had big plans.

"Hopefully, not while I'm alive. I am recommending that you
undergo psychiatric evaluation and dismissal."

Psychiatry and dismissal. Tanchester was not surprised. The
dean, no doubt, was part of the conspiracy, probably a ringleader.
Tanchester, a tie hanging out of his pants pocket and a bundle
of clothes tucked under his arm, explained that to his classmate,

Charlie Crawford, as he marched from Rhodeway's office to the hospital.

"The man is a demented bag of wind."

"I guess your meeting didn't go smoothly," Crawford concluded.

"Time for action," Elville whispered hoarsely. "TJ2376M."

"TJ...eh.....6M?"

"That's Rhodeway's computer access code."

"That's nice," Crawford said, turning sharply and bounding down the stairs.

Five minutes later, on what would soon be known in Mid-Atlantic Hospital as

'Super Glitch Tuesday', Elville Tanchester was in the computer room in the back of 6 South. Compared to recreating the world properly, which he would have to defer, Plan B was going to be simple.

He sat down at the small desk and pulled his chair up to the monitor, straightened the keypad, punched into the system with Rhodeway's access code, and grabbed the light pen from its holder. He chose "Patient by Alphabetical Listing". A-Am. Up came: Abelman, Joseph. MAH 00098732

> Room 327   Dr. B. Phillips
> Select
> > A. New Orders
> > B. Review Orders
> > C. Laboratory
> > D. Discharge
> > E. Everything Else

Elville zapped Discharge and then added "Now" when a second message flashed on the screen. On to the next name. Abingwicker, gone. Accochio, gone. Twenty-three minutes, forty-five seconds later James J. Zunderlilly disappeared. Every patient in every bed had been paraded across the screen and discharged – NOW. The census, 343 when he logged in, was zero. Except for dancing paramecia, the screen was subdued and blank.

Smiling, he put the light pen down just as Karen Stillwell, another senior, pushed the door open and headed for the computer. Stillwell was wearing a short white jacket. Elville had always meant to buy one of those.

"What are you doing here?" Tanchester asked.

"I'm assigned to this floor. What are YOU doing here?"

"TJ2376M," he shot back.

"TJ23…7..M?" Stillwell repeated. But why would she question this classmate.

"Are you finished?" she asked, inching toward the keyboard. "I need to punch a few orders in on one of my patients."

Elville got up and stepped aside. Karen sat down, hit some keys, lifted the light pen and pushed again. "Shit." She ran her fingers through her hair and frowned. With her mouth and forehead twisted, except for not being bald, she looked a lot like the dean.

"You seem upset," Tanchester observed.

"Shit. I can't bring my patient's name up on the screen." She picked up the keypad and dropped it on the table. "We have rounds with Phillips in five minutes." She typed the student code again. Nothing on the monitor. "I'm dead."

"Don't waste your time. Your patient's been discharged."

"Adele Trucker? No she hasn't. I just came from her room. 619. She has two I.V. lines, a Foley catheter and a naso-gastric tube. She's not going anywhere."

"Right, she is not going anywhere, but she has been discharged. I just discharged her between Torweiss and Tuckton. Martin Tuckton, room 418."

Stillwell squeezed the light pen and eyed her classmate.

"You can't write any orders," he told her. "According to the computer, your patient is gone. According to the admissions office, she is gone. They should be filling her bed soon."

"It is filled, She's still in the damn bed, airhead."

"Right," Elville agreed. "But the clerks are about to send someone up to her room and to every bed in the hospital. That's their job. You're going to have a lot of workups tonight. I'm glad I'm not on call."

"How is Mrs. Trucker going to get her meds?"

"The pharmacy thinks she's gone. And the solution room won't be sending up any I.V. fluids, either." Tanchester, satisfied with step one, threw the computer manual in the air and tried to catch it. It hit Stillwell's right foot.

"Karen, everything stops when a patient's discharge is punched in."

"But why Mrs. Trucker? Why did you pick my patient?" Stillwell's tone, while she hopped on one leg, was more desperate.

"They're all gone. I discharged everyone. No pills, no blood, no low sodium chicken salad, no surgical instruments, no x-rays. Everything is on hold."

"You're a mad man," she cried. "Why did you do this?"

"Why do people climb Mount Everest?"

He walked out of the room and down the stairs. His wide-eyed classmate, mouth hanging open, followed mutely. As they walked toward the 5 South nurses station, a cluster of nurses, aides and a clerk ran by, screaming at each other and throwing sheets and towels. They seemed especially worried about the elderly men and women, admission papers and suitcases on their laps, waiting at the front desk in wheel chairs.

Tanchester and Stillwell darted around the chairs and on to 5 North, where the intern, Jumbo Jack Urbane, was banging on the computer keyboard with his reflex hammer and cursing. "This damn system is supposed to be idiot proof."

"It is idiot proof," Tanchester explained to his classmate as they walked past Jumbo Jack, "but I'm not an idiot. And it's not tamper proof."

"Tanchester, STOP THIS!" Karen screamed.

"And anyone with the ability to put a tie on can switch every patient's medications, or lab reports, or doctor." Tanchester's eyes rolled up. "And anyone can discover little things about patients and sell the information to the highest bidder; who's eating roach powder, who's pregnant, who's got the clap."

Karen, breathing noisily, didn't seem to care.

"Did you know that there was an 87 year-old former governor in 317 who just had a vasectomy?"

No. She didn't know that. Was it going to be on the urology exam?

"It doesn't really matter. I just discharged him."

"Tanchester!" Karen grabbed his shoulders and shoved him against the wall.

"Some people have too much faith in defective information feedback systems. I tried telling that to the old skinhead," Tanchester continued. "This should teach him a lesson."

Of course it would. Stillwell admitted that she had learned a lesson, too. Now, would he stop the crap and straighten everything out?

"That part is not easy," he explained. "Every patient needs a hospital number and will have to be processed through the admissions office again. All the orders and the lab reports and the plans for surgery have been wiped out and will have to be reordered when the patients get new numbers. That will take awhile."

"Well, start right away, "Karen pleaded.

"That may not be possible," Tanchester explained calmly. "A lot of the beds have already been given away. Remember the old Mid-Atlantic motto: "Every empty bed is an ugly sore on the backside of our hospital."

Karen had heard enough. She dashed away from her smiling classmate and headed for the administrative wing. "Stay right there. Don't move." She would explain the problem.

She didn't have to explain. Everyone in the director's office knew. Dean Rhodeway denied, during cross-examination, that he had tampered with the computer. In the first place, he had no motive and furthermore, he had been in his office all afternoon, trying to clean it up and get the smell out.

"Well, who had access to your computer number?"

The dean had someone in mind. Two guards with handcuffs and a squadron of psychiatric social workers were dispatched to arrest one Elville M. Tanchester.

Dennis Lipsink, hospital president, marched back and forth. "Cattleman, you convinced me that this was the perfect data system for Mid-Atlantic. Now what am I going to tell the board of directors and Channel 9 news?"

"Well, uh, until today we had only seven and a half erroneous discharges in five years with the Hosp-Info-Super Data II," Irv Cattleman, Vice-president of Information explained. "And we get beautiful four-color graphics."

Cattleman stood below his diplomas and a framed sign: "There are no computer errors – only human errors".

"Seven and a half discharges," Lipsink screamed. "That sounds great for the annual report, but right now this place is wild."

"Wild," Nan Haggeston, Vice president of Nursing, repeated. "We've got a spleen hanging half out in O.R. 3 because the supply room won't release a Steinstoner retractor to the circulating nurse. The clerk can't punch the patient number in because the guy was discharged while Dr. Hartack was cutting through his rectus abdominus muscle. The clerk said she wouldn't issue equipment without a charge number and lose her job just because some stupid nurse is on her knees begging and crying. 'Screw the nurse. Rules are rules', she said."

"Rules are rules," Cattleman agreed. He outlined the problem to the hospital president and to Haggeston and to Mark Clayton, a reporter from the Herald Examiner who walked into the Information Office, pushing a wheelchair partially filled with his crying mother. Mother Clayton had been discharged from 3 West approximately nine minutes after being admitted for a transverse colon polypectomy.

Mother Clayton was still in her slip and one stocking. "Is this a new length-of-stay record for your hospital?" the reporter asked. "You must be quite proud."

"I don't know what to do," Cattleman confessed. "I trained everyone to look at the screens. Now I'm an information expert with no information."

As Cattleman backed into a corner, his office filled with more reporters, Mark Baker of News at 5, some doctors, a few hungry patients and an old gentleman from 2 East who had just had a little accident. It happens now and then. All he needed was a clean pair of pajamas. Medium. Any color would be fine.

His secretary asked if Mr. Cattleman would please pick up extension 23. Mr. Blake Danielson, founder of the Garfield City Sprinkler Valve Company, second lieutenant under Douglas MacArthur in the Big War, and chairman of the hospital board of directors, was on the line. He didn't have any questions, but he wanted answers.

"Yes, sir, I have the answers," Irv declared into the telephone. His face was wet and shiny. "Lots of answers, Mr. Danielson. But they are in the computer."

The Mid-Atlantic Hospital Board of Directors meets in the imposing 14th floor conference room, the mahogany morgue, on the third Thursday of every month. There were 18 items on the agenda for the February meeting, but the members, with dark eyes and darker suits, wanted to discuss just two: Item #7 – State of the Art Computer Patient Interfacing and Modern Health Care Delivery and #12 – lunch.

Irv Cattleman, President Lipsink and Vice-President Haggeston looked into the close-mouthed lined faces of the stiff bodies. Chairman Danielson, banging his riding crop on the table, reminded the officers that this was not an inquisition. He would think of a stronger word later.

Happily, Lipsink, backing away from the prod swaying in front of his nose, could report that the effects of that little computer glitch were totally corrected…"in part due to an abrupt, unexplained, decline in the number of patients on the admissions waiting list."

"And what about that sinister left-wing information radical?"

Lipsink believed that Mr. Tanchester was safely tucked away in the Psychiatric Unit. "He seemed frustrated by his inability to discharge himself, but otherwise appears quite reflective."

"I guess we taught him a lesson," Danielson replied.

Lipsink started to smile, but quit in the middle.

Cattleman explained that the annoying glitch in the system had been removed. Patients could be discharged only by their attending physician and two consenting adults. Two armed guards and a picture of Tanchester are posted at each computer terminal. Along with a pit bull.

Danielson thanked Cattleman and the officers. He agreed that this problem would never happen again. "You see, I have an idea that will revolutionize the entire health and disease industry. I call it the Human Touch System, the Danielson Human Touch System." He banged the table with his crop. "Once we get the details ironed out, we will have our people talking to other people and not little pink screens."

The administrators seemed confused.

"The screens are green," Cattleman whispered to Lipsink.

"An admissions clerk will walk from unit to unit to see which patients are leaving and which beds are actually empty. She will make direct eye contact with the mattresses. The Danielson Direct Eye Contact Method. If she's not on coffee break, she might even say good-bye to some of the departing patients."

Cattleman's mouth dropped. This revealed an entire new facet of the chairman's mind.

"Real clerks will pick up the phone and talk to other real clerks to schedule tests," the chairman continued. "The pharmacists will visit the patient floors and discuss pills with the nurses. I see an entire hospital of people talking to people. The Blake Danielson Direct Communication People to People System of America."

"Brilliant," Nurse Haggeston shouted.

"Eventually, we can teach x-ray technicians how to smile and lab techs how to talk."

"Hmm. It just might work," President Lipsink agreed.

"A model for other hospitals," Haggeston added.

"The screens are green," Cattleman whispered again.

"This is my baby," Danielson beamed. "And I have just hired a most remarkable young man to run it. He has a unique background in medical care and some refreshing ideas." The board chairman stood. "The fellow wears peculiar ties and may not look like the corporate type, but he is going to turn this place around." The crop was swaying in front of Lipsink's face again. "I know you will all give him your full cooperation."

HELP, I CAN'T GET IN!

"That's nine," Nurse Loretta shouted as the ambulance zipped past Dexter Memorial Hospital. Baptist Medical had been number eight. "Hurry, or this guy ain't gonna make it."

"Look, this stiff is a SuperHealthy member, and we've gotta take him to a SuperHealthy Hospital." Dave Markham, the crew chief, said nothing more as he watched the Chicago skyline recede in the side-view mirror. He straddled the patient, pumping a rubber bag twelve times a minute.

Two hundred twenty pumps later, a tower with a large "**P-S-G**" on the roof rose from the center of a dark clump of houses. A second billboard on the same tower acknowledged that Paid Subscriber General Hospital was "A Member of the SuperHealthy Family – Serves You Right."

The ambulance made it to the driveway, and the stiff still had a pulse. The road signs were clear: Main Entrance to the right, Advertising and Marketing straight ahead, and Emergencies to the left. Jimmy, the driver, turned left. But the road turned right and then left and left again before it reached the front entrance. Or was it the back? The ambulance faced a brick wall.

The stiff, some guy named Charlie, flopping over the sides of the stretcher, had looked good when they picked him up. Now he was gray and limp. The beat on the monitor was slow, then rapid, then slow again as the van started another loop around the damn building.

Paid Subscriber General Hospital had won the 2003 Medical Architecture Design Award, but in the dark it looked more like a war memorial or a giant syringe on end than a hospital.

"Dammit," Jimmy howled, "this place is a friggin' fortress." On the third try he spotted an opening in a clump of sandalwood trees. He turned sharply and saw a small sign with smaller letters: EME G NCY.

The ambulance raced down a dark narrow ramp. Loretta and Jimmy ripped the doors open and pulled the stretcher into the EME G NCY room. "Got a bad one for you," Loretta shouted. One minute and 42 seconds later, the pasty SuperHealthy subscriber had a seizure and his heart stopped beating.

"Medicine is a great institution," Charles Campfield, a board certified architect, had proclaimed six years earlier, finger in the air, as he practiced his sales pitch. "A great industry to work in. Make that 'in which to work.'"

"In simpler times," he continued, warming to the subject, "the family physician, the GP, with his warm smile and black bag, was the institution of medicine. After being led to the sickbed by a worried woman in a floral apron, the benign gray-haired healer wasted little time before inspecting the tongue, jabbing a thermometer under it and a pine stick over it. 'Say aaaah.' Perhaps a doctor's greatest fear – his nightmare – was being awakened in the middle of the night to minister to a tongueless patient."

His wife, Anne, thought that this comment was irrelevant and really quite stupid, but Charlie wanted to begin with a bit of levity.

"Finally, when he had milked that versatile oral body part for all it could offer, the doctor reached into his bag, pulled out a syringe and administered a quick cure without informed consent or waivers. Then, all he had to do was close his bag, refuse a nice cup of coffee, put the six dollars in his pocket and get back into his Oldsmobile. The accounts receivable department was in his hip pocket, and he had no line item for advertising. Quaint. Thank God that things aren't like that anymore."

Campfield was certain that the statement would impress the SuperHealthy officers. It put his design for the new Garfield City Subscriber Hospital – Garf-Med – into proper perspective.

A week later, as Charlie paced the hall awaiting the call, an invitation vibrated through the door. Was it from a woman with laryngitis or a hormonally distressed male? Inside the conference room, Marty Phelps, Jane Rodgers and Glen Adamowicz of the home office were seated at the table, submerged in reams of cost analyses and demographics and a pile of cigarette butts. There was no room for tongue blades or thermometers, but the architect found a few square feet on the corner of the table to roll out his plans – which he did with the flair of a Persian rug merchant, despite Ann's warning to be subtle.

"I give you the definitive health care facility. It will be a model for the entire industry," Charles proclaimed. His preamble about oral appendages was forgotten.

The executives stared at the white lines on the blue paper, and then at the young Garfield City architect.

"What is this monster going to cost?" Jane Rodgers asked. She was vice-president in charge of money. Her "to-the-point" attitude was reinforced by her buttoned-down blue Oxford shirt and yellow tie.

"Right, Chuckie," Glen Adamowicz added. "We've priced these babies out in forty urban markets, and you've got to bring it in below $260 million or we'll use the Plattsville plans."

"I don't have a final figure on construction costs yet," Campfield sputtered. "But cost isn't everything."

"Cost isn't everything?" Rodgers repeated slowly, letting the strange words roll around her mouth like a clump of rocks.

"Right. This is a totally new concept for a hospital," Campfield explained. "The physical structure is designed to enhance the primary goal of the GarfMed division."

"The BOTTOM LINE!" the team shouted.

"Right, the bottom line." Campfield pulled a sheet from the plans. "This is the vertical elevation. The surface is composed entirely of alternating blue and red windows."

"Nope. No windows," Marty Phelps shouted. "It increases air-conditioning cost in summer and heating in winter." Phelps, Super-Healthy's director of engineering, pushed his chair back and stood. "In the Vermont unit we have a 250,000 square foot building with just one window ....in the treasurer's office. In Wisconsin, the entire thing is underground."

"I understand," Charlie had to admit. "But you're losing sight of one important fact. What is the single largest item in the budget of each of your facilities?"

"Those DAMN MEDICAL COSTS," the big shots sang out.

"Right. And although my architectural plan is not energy-efficient, it *will* cut medical costs."

"Stop right there," Phelps interrupted. "My staff has looked at every scheme for cutting medical costs. I doubt that a local architect can come up with a structural innovation that will save us money."

"Well, I have," Charlie beamed. "Look at this vertical elevation. There are 720 windows and just one three-foot glass door. The efficiency of the plan lies in the location and design of the door. And the windows are just camouflage. The principle is simple; I'm surprised that no one thought of it earlier. You see," he continued, "your average cost for a single hospital day is $18,572.54. With standard operational efficiencies, you can cut that by six or seven percent."

"We're shooting for nine point four," Adamowicz rebutted.

"That's great," Campfield acknowledged. "However, as a contract organization, your real savings come from decreasing the number of admissions of subscribers. If the patient doesn't come in, you save the entire cost."

"Naturally, we try to enroll only healthy people, and we've tried preventive medicine plans," Adamowicz retaliated. "No salt, low-fat, no smoking, strong condoms, vitamins, exercise. But they actually *increase* the number of hospital days."

"Hmm," Rogers conceded.

"That sounds right," Phelps admitted. "But, no doors? What about building codes and fire regulations?"

"No problem," Charles replied. "The regulations only require *exits*. The building will have exits: large one-way ports. It will be easy to leave. I'm sure you have no objection to that."

"What about the workers?"

"That's easy, too," Campfield comforted them. "The employees will know where the door is hidden. They just have to be sure no one is watching when they sneak in."

Phelps wondered if it would be time-consuming to have the workers sneak into the hospital. Campfield assured him that the delay would be insignificant – since the staff could be quite small, and would have nothing to do if the patients couldn't find the door.

"Sounds okay to me." Phelps was convinced. "But what if they *do* find the door?"

Campfield pulled a report from his computer case. "There are 12 potential door sites, and the door will be switched every time someone finds it. And it will have no handle." Campfield held up a small door. It looked like a dark window.

"YES! Your plan will revolutionize health care," Adamowicz agreed. "The banks will be beating down our door…. if they can find it."

Marty Phelps was still not convinced. "Cost *efficiency* is not the bottom line, and saving bucks is not the bottom line. Aren't you overlooking the need to provide service?"

"Provide service?" Jane's and Gene's faces flushed.

"Right. The primary goal of a first-rate medical facility is not cost cutting," Phelps continued. "Or attracting investors."

"It's not?"

"No. The real goal is *selling subscriptions*. And if we don't provide at least some care, we'll lose customers. The public can be quite fickle."

"On the surface that sounds sensible," Adamowicz rebutted. "But it's not. If we sold policies to individuals, or if we sold cars or apples, we would have to cater to the consumer. But we sell to business and industry – and they are on our side. Since health care is part of their benefit package, they want the cheapest product and now we can give it to them."

No one could find a flaw in that argument. The ecstatic Super-Healthy executives predicted that some day Charlie's design concept would be the model for the industry. He would do to health care what dynamite had done to warfare.

Before long, the prediction came true. The Garf-Med plan became the prototype for every new facility in the world's fastest growing medical corporation. Charles Campfield was hailed as the father of Limited Access Design, and, over time, he unveiled plans for moats, blind tunnels, drawbridges and armed turrets.

His picture was on the cover of *Newsfront*. And six years later Campfield was on the podium in the Chicago Loop Hotel to accept the Austin Ledbetter Award of the American Institute of Medical Architects and Designers.

That was a great evening for Anne and Charles Campfield – one of drinking, dancing and dreaming. In his euphoria, arms waving, he declared that nothing could stop him. However, ten minutes later a pain in the chest did. Anne pulled a chair over and sat him down. When his denials became slurred, Anne went for help and Charles was strapped in an ambulance and sent on his way to Paid Subscriber General Hospital, one of his shiny new glass cubes.

The ambulance crew, finally reaching the hospital, had even more trouble finding the emergency entrance. Charlie looked like a limp rag, and it took the doctors and nurses 20 minutes to get his heart going.

"But thank God," Anne said. "They saved him." Well, sorta.

The man, his age hard to guess, was held back by a sheet tied around his waist and the chair. The name on the door was Charles Campfield, but the nurse called him Charlie Boy and complained that after six years, she was tired of cleaning up his mess. His sounds — "bbbe.......bbe.....bbe...." - were hardly a response, and they continued after the nurse had left. Charlie Boy's eyes looked past the bed and the TV. A bit of milky broth dribbled out of the tube pinned to his robe that trailed out of his nose.

A single sheet of paper lay on Charlie's bedside table. It was not a menu; he did not select his meals. And it was not a TV schedule. It looked like a computer printout with columns and numbers. And stamped diagonally across the sheet in red block letters was the message:

Paid in Full
A.P. SuperHealthy America
Jane Rodgers, Treasurer

WOW! WHAT A LIABILITY

"Are you Lloyd W. Cincheck, 565 Lionshare Terrace, Garfield City?"

"Of course, I am," Lloyd answered. He then heard a voice in the back of the room whisper that this was quite a posh address for a night shift blackjack dealer. Lee Montgomery Montgomery, the plaintiff's attorney, undoubtedly agreed. And he must have liked the Mercedes sedan and twenty-seven foot Boston Whaler in the driveway.

"Do you swear to tell the truth, the whole……"

Lloyd certainly would try.

"Lloyd Cincheck, you have been charged with trespassing. How do you plead?"

"Not guilty."

"You have been further charged with the unauthorized, callous administration of hazardous pharmaceutical agents to an unwilling subject in a public place. How do you plead?"

"Not guilty."

"And practicing medicine without a license. And violating the civil rights of a very nice man."

"Definitely not guilty, Your Honor."

The judge then nodded to a man who looked like he had just swallowed a peeled lemon. The deep-lined, sour faced man pushed his chair back, stood slowly, and, with deliberate steps, walked across the room.

"Is this your statement?" Jim Hoffmeister's lemon faced attorney asked as he handed Lloyd a three-inch stack of fuzzy printouts.

The blackjack dealer, without responding, examined the papers as sweat stained his black suit and wilted the collar of his white shirt. Although he had saved this suit for Amy's wedding, Brick Weiman, his lawyer, told him to wear it to the hearing or there might not be a wedding.

On the night of the incident, Lloyd had been in his clown outfit: red pants, red bowtie and a frilly yellow vest with daisies, butterflies and pregnant bumble bees. Hoffmeister, the large plaintiff, was not somber, sober, righteous, wronged James J. Hoffmeister then. He was 'Jim Baby'. He was the shiny-headed player in seat four, behind heavy dark cigar smoke. Before the alleged assault, Hoffmeister had managed to spill two drinks and lose seven thousand four hundred dollars and his loud sense of humor in twenty minutes of heavy bets and plain bad luck.

That night, a typical winter Tuesday, Cincheck was standing behind table BJ-14, trying to look as rigid, non-threatening and bored as he had been taught to look in Lucky Lou's eight week, twelve hundred dollar dealer's course. 'Jim Baby' was the only action, and Lloyd, the clown, tried to focus on the 1888 presidential campaign for his term paper. Where had Grover Cleveland made his mistake?

One hundred and twenty years later, younger and less presidential, Lila Clarke sat behind Jim Hoffmeister. She was not yet coy Lila, the reluctant eyewitness. She was dark-rooted, blonde Lila with rhinestone-studded finger nails and significantly oversized contents of an undersized red dress. Lloyd hadn't thought that she was Jim's wife and knew that she wasn't his daughter.

Today, in the judge's walnut-paneled room, nine miles from the casino, there were no cocktail waitresses or Frank Sinatra CDs; and 'Jim Baby' was sitting next to a smiling lady in a brown flowered dress and a black sweater. She could have been Lila's mother, but clearly was not. Ms. Lila R. Clarke, licensed recreational therapist, sat alone in the last row of the chamber, head down in dark glasses and a six or seven piece green and gray suit.

During what proved to be the final hand, the dealer (aka defendant), with one hidden card, had a five displayed. The plaintiff had a pair of threes, which he split, doubling his five hundred dollar bet.

Lloyd turned the page. The statement noted that "the player seemed pale and jittery, while his companion was quite calm. She squeezed the plaintiff on his right thigh; and, as Jim pushed the chips forward, Lila searched for some hair on the back of his head to stroke. The dealer drew a card from the shoe and placed it on the first three. It was an eight, giving the player eleven."

"I got ya now," the played yelled, banging the table. His eyes brightened. He smiled at his companion, shoved his soggy cigar into his mouth and dropped five more black chips next to the cards.

"Gimme a picture," Hoffmeister shouted. Lila wrapped her arms around Jim's chest and wiggled her soft parts against his back.

"I slipped the next card out," Cincheck read, "and flipped it in place."

"A ten!" 'Jim Baby' screamed.

No. It was the five of hearts. Lila released Jim's torso.

"As the card hit the table, the player raised his lips toward his bulbous nose and peered at me as though I had just urinated in his scotch and soda. I hadn't."

The report noted that a small crowd had gathered to watch the action and look down Lila's dress.

"Without delay, I moved to the next hand and dropped an eight on the second three. 'Jim Baby' pushed a thumb in the air and added five hundred dollars to his second promising eleven. From a once enviable multicolored stack, only a single green chip and two red ones remained. Thirty five bucks."

"You owe me one," the player yelled hoarsely.

The dealer drew a five from the shoe and tossed it on the cards. The once promising pile of chips stood behind two pathetic sixteens with no opportunity for improvement.

The eyes of the crowd now moved from Lila's pair to the dealer's. If Cincheck didn't bust, Jim was wiped out. Cincheck turned up his down card, indifferent to the player's stare. The pit boss, equally indifferent, looked over the dealer's shoulder and into the pearl necklace dangling in Lila's cleavage.

The audience formed a tightly packed semi-circle, four rows deep. Cincheck pulled a card from the shoe and flipped it. The flipped card, now resting next to the dealer's five, was a dour queen of clubs in a red Elizabethan gown, elegant but quite unlike Lila's. The house, with fifteen, had to draw another card. The odds were with 'Jim Baby'.

Lila squeezed Hoffmeister's left thigh, perhaps a promise of good times as soon as the dealer busted. The hushed crowd stiffened as Lloyd drew a card and dropped it gently on the waiting queen.

"Bust," someone in row three shouted. "Pull a big one. Hit a brick."

The card, falling on the queen was not a brick or a big one. It was the six of spades. The dealer, Lloyd W. Cincheck, agent of the Grand Garfield Casino, had twenty-one.

"Mr. Hoffmeister shook his scowling head wildly and pulled his shoulders back," Cincheck continued reading, "perhaps to signal to Lila to pull her claws out of his abundant extremities. I drew the cards and his chips back in a single motion. In response, the player raised his right arm and opened his mouth to speak. Nothing. Not a single syllable or grunt emerged. He curled his beefy hands into fists and pressed them firmly into the center of his chest. His eyes rolled upward, his ashen head dropped back, his stool flipped over and the high roller rolled onto his face on the plush purple carpet with circles of gold stars."

As the plaintiff's attorney stood overhead, Cincheck nodded. Yes, this was his report. He thought that his observations were precise and well written.

At that moment, according to his statement and the word of nineteen eye witnesses, Cincheck leaped over the table, rolled the whale-like form onto his back and shouted for the crowd to call fire-rescue. But the crowd scattered as the hand that had just dealt himself twenty-one pounded on the lifeless chest. He then pinched the bulbous veiny nose, tilted the head back, and breathed into the victim's purple, cigar-stained mouth. He was quickly joined by a man who proudly proclaimed his knowledge of cardiac resuscitation.

"Hi, I'm Billy, and I know CPR."

"I'm Lloyd, and I know all the American vice-presidents," Cincheck panted.

The pair worked rhythmically until three men and a woman in white coveralls and blue baseball caps rushed through the casino doors to the blackjack table with all the action. Lloyd explained the events in short breathless sentences as he wiped his mouth and assisted in connecting the EKG wires and IV tubing.

"I'm Billy, and I know CPR," Cincheck's partner repeated.

"Keep compressing his chest, Billy," someone urged.

"One c.c. of intracardiac epinephrine," Lloyd shouted as he looked at the green EKG screen with a yellow straight line.

The two men in white next to the equipment looked at each other and then at Lloyd's flowered yellow and black vest without responding to the dealer's command.

"Give me the damn epinephrine!"

"That's a good idea. Give it to the dealer," the third man ordered.

Following the injection, the yellow line on the green screen bounced up and down wildly.

"Great, we've got ventricular fibrillation. Let's shock him and give him an amp of bicarb and some calcium," Cincheck shouted again.

"Yes, sir. I'm getting the defibrillator ready," the third man indicated and handed a pair of steel paddles to the medic next to 'Jim Baby's' chest. When the red button was pushed, Jim's chest and shoulders bounced up, his head hit the CPR board and the yellow line turned to a wavy pattern. Lloyd and the team in blue hats smiled. So did the pit boss.

"I'm getting a pulse," one of the medics proclaimed, his hand not far from Lila's favorite spot. A loud cheer erupted from the crowd as Jim's arms and legs moved wildly. He was breathing. Those who came for casino action seemed to be satisfied.

"I'm getting a blood pressure. Let's get him out of here." The team lifted Hoffmeister onto a stretcher and rushed their equipment and their patient out of the casino and into a Mid-Atlantic ambulance as, overhead, Frank Sinatra sang "I Did It My Way." At the same time the dealer clipped his red bow tie, straightened his vest, suspenders and cummerbund, and stepped behind the blackjack table, counting the chips, as the crowd applauded and shouted for a bow. A woman in a pink ribbon and red tutu walked through the crowd with a small tray and note pad, taking drink orders.

"Is this the man that you pounced on and into whom you injected foreign substances?" Lee Montgomery Montgomery, Hoffmeister's attorney asked, placing his hand on his client's shoulder. The plaintiff's black suit and black tie were darker than Lloyd's, and he wore a shiny gray shirt like the one that the defendant had ripped off his lifeless chest two and a half years earlier.

Grace Hoffmeister, a smiling, plump figure with large sagging breasts and white, curly hair sat next to her husband. She clutched a brown pocketbook and not his thigh.

"Yes, he is the man," Cincheck answered over his attorney's objections about foreign substances and other maliciously chosen participles and verbs.

"Are you a blackjack dealer in the Grand Garfield Casino?"

"Yes, night shift and week-ends."

"Do your duties as a dealer include mouth-to-mouth resuscitation, chest compression and intra-cardiac injections?"

"No."

Montgomery Montgomery smiled. "Do you consider yourself qualified in these procedures, and can you recognize a person in need of these life saving measures? The diagnosis of death is not easy to establish."

"The plaintiff's lips were purple, he had no heart beat, and he wasn't breathing," Lloyd responded. "I took those to be bad signs."

"Do you consider yourself skilled in life-supporting maneuvers?" Montgomery Montgomery's questions seemed to rise from his long slender nose.

"Yes, I do."

"And where, sir, in the gaming industry did you develop these sophisticated diagnostic and therapeutic skills?" The lemon-faced lawyer's words were coming out faster, louder and two octaves higher.

"At the Garfield University College of Medicine and the University and Mid-Atlantic Hospitals," the defendant responded slowly and flatly.

Suddenly the only sound in the room came from the reams of papers that Hoffmeister's lawyer tossed around the table, over his shoulder and at his feet.

"He was going for the quick buck, again, and didn't do his homework," Brick Weiman whispered to his client. "He liked your assets."

"I see," Montgomery Montgomery stammered. "Are you a..... eh....are you...you're not a doctor, are you?"

"I am," the dealer responded.

"Let the record show," Weiman indicated, "that the defendant graduated Magna Cum Laude from Garfield University College of Medicine in 1984 and is board certified in Internal Medicine and Cardiology. Let the record further show that he was an Associate Professor of Medicine at Garfield University Hospital until his appointment as Director of the Division of Cardiology at Mid-Atlantic Medical College and Hospital in 2002."

Weiman then walked to the chair where Hoffmeister's attorney was slumped and dropped fourteen pounds of papers on his lap, along with a series of crumbs that inadvertently fell from his stringy salt and pepper beard. "I thought that you might want to review some of my client's journal articles," the defense counsel added. He did not mention the textbook, <u>Diagnosis and Treatment of Valvular Heart Disease</u>.

After a few moments of silence, Montgomery Montgomery was granted a short recess.

Unfortunately for the plaintiff and his counsel, following the break the defendant was still a physician. None-the-less, Mr. Montgomery Montgomery, running his fingers through his shiny black hair, started a line of questioning that seemed to restore his color and confidence.

"Does it seem a bit odd that you, a distinguished physician, would give up your long medical career to become a nightshift blackjack dealer?"

"No."

"Is it not true, DOCtor Cincheck, that you are no longer practicing medicine because you are unable to get malpractice insurance?"

"No, it is not true," the cardiologist replied. "I can get coverage for fifty seven thousand dollars a year. But frankly, in my practice, with primarily indigent patients, I cannot afford to pay that much."

"Isn't it true," Montgomery Montgomery, teeth shining, continued, "that your rates went up because of the incredible number of liability suits that you lost?"

"No."

"NO?" Saliva was dripping down Montgomery Montgomery's chin. "What about Novack v. Cincheck and Garrison v. Morshack, Cincheck and Pyle? What about Hartman v. Pyle, Boust, Wineberg, Cincheck, et.al?"

"What about Lowell v. Gates and Cincheck or Tremont v. Cincheck and the Commonwealth of Pennsylvania?" The man in pinstripes seemed to have gotten quite a bit smarter in just twenty minutes.

"And Glover v. Cincheck and Garfield University Hospital?" Montgomery Montgomery inhaled and deflated slowly.

"You forgot Ardrissian v. Cincheck," the cardiologist added helpfully.

Weiman clapped his hands over Cincheck's mouth.

"Seven cases in eight years," Montgomery Montgomery rose from his chair and shouted, pointing toward the ceiling. "Perhaps a new indoor record for the state. Doesn't that give the court a clear indication of your medical judgment, ability and competence, DOCtor?"

"No," Cincheck repeated. He hadn't been called doctor like that since his junior year rotation on obstetrics. "No, I won them all. When you take another recess, counselor, you will find that I won all seven. My total liability loss was much less than your client left on the table when he keeled over."

The plaintiff's attorney sat back and looked up. He appeared to be pushing his tongue meekly through his thin lips.

"One case was dropped because I was in San Francisco at the time that I should have been killing Norton Novack in Garfield City."

"An honest administrative mistake," Montgomery Montgomery added to the record.

"In three cases," Cincheck continued, "I was named by attorneys who copied every name on the chart that they could read. I was guilty of good penmanship."

"If that is true, doctor, why were you denied standard, cheap coverage?"

"Too much action."

"Too much action?" Montgomery Montgomery questioned.

"Insurance companies, counselor, hate to spend money and, win or lose, it costs a lot to process a suit. If your name comes up often on their computer, you are out. And you may have noticed that some folks are doing a lot of suing these days?"

"That is interesting, but not relevant to…."

Montgomery Montgomery's rejoinder was interrupted by a loud thud against the wooden floor, and all heads turned to a soft, round, body that was sprawled under an overturned mahogany chair.

"For an adult that guy spends a lot of time under chairs," Cincheck whispered to his lawyer.

The bulky mass, with an ashen face and purple lips, was clutching his chest. Foam bubbled out of his mouth, and his eyes, Hoffmeister's eyes, rolled up. Suddenly his legs jerked and his body stretched out, flaccid and lifeless.

"HELP! HELP him," Grace screamed and fainted. Lila Clark took off her shoes and ran from the room. The nineteen casino witnesses, pale and motionless in the last three rows, watched something strangely familiar.

"Call 911", Lloyd shouted, and Weiman pulled out his cell phone and dialed.

Cincheck, looking at his lawyer, shook his head and sighed. He then jumped over the table, kicked a chair and scattered papers across the floor. He then shifted Hoffmeister's head and pulled his mouth open and cleared it with his index finger. Montgomery Montgomery, perhaps with a new understanding of 'trespassing', looked both frightened and ashamed, as Cincheck, once again, checked for a pulse and pressed down on the plaintiff's chest.

THERE IS A TIME

When the doors flew open, the noisy hoard, many in dirty white jackets and blood-stained, floppy green pants, circled the nurses' station and overran the Medical ICU. Wednesday renal rounds had started. As two aides jumped back and fell into a linen cart, the unrelenting column spilled down the hallway, squeezed through a doorway and disappeared into room 512. Once inside the windowless, green-tiled room, Dave Ferguson, the senior nephrology fellow, led Professor Phillips, a stooped gray-haired figure, to the foot of the bed. Residents and students scurried into crevices between the bed, the walls and the chrome and plastic pumps, motors and monitors. A few students dangled from hangers on the coat rack.

Ferguson opened the patient's chart and coughed, a signal to the undulating bodies surrounding the bed to secure their clipboards and shut up. The beep of monitors and the hissing of a ventilator suggested that somewhere in the middle there was a patient. The card read **Agnes Mulligan**.

The senior fellow opened the chart and raised his chin to its full anatomical limit. "The patient is a one hundred and three year old white female who developed acute renal failure following cardiac by-pass surgery." The stooped figure to his right, Burton Phillips, the Leland Snodsmith Professor of Medicine and Director of the Division of Nephrology, peered between the dialysis equipment and the cardiac monitor to the head of the bed. The patient's face was totally obscured by a tangle of I.V. lines and monitor wires. The endotracheal tube dipped down between the sheets and disappeared.

"Mrs. A.M. was in good health until thirty-four years age when she developed right-sided weakness and slurred speech following a stroke. Over the next fifteen years she had seven heart attacks, three episodes of G.I. bleeding and a ruptured abdominal aortic aneurysm." Ferguson spoke slowly. He did not mention the previous cancer surgery or the occasional amputation of an extremity or other equally withered body part.

Phillips wondered if Mrs. A.M. is the famous old Agnes Mulligan whose husband never returned from Stuttgart after the war to end all wars.

"In January cardiac cath demonstrated significant narrowing in all coronary arteries, and the patient was prepped for by-pass surgery," Ferguson added.

The division director expressed surprise that she had any arteries left to narrow. No one smiled. Therefore, he decided not to ask why anyone would catheterize a lady who was born when Grover Cleveland was still the struggling mayor of Buffalo. (1)

"Following surgery the patient could not be weaned from the ventilator because of pre-existing chronic obstructive lung disease," Ferguson continued. "Two days later, A.M. had a cardiac arrest. She was successfully resuscitated and has been unresponsive since then."

The Leland Snodsmith Professor pointed out the often imprecise definition of "success" while squinting at the lumpy quivering form under the covers.

"The patient subsequently developed pneumonia and sepsis. Following several courses of antibiotics, her urine output decreased, and on August 14th we were called to evaluate the situation."

Everyone, except the professor, smiled.

"The studies were consistent with acute renal failure, and we started dialysis on August 16th."

The chief turned toward the bed again. A blanket covered the bumps and mounds, and he could not find the dear old face. "Did anyone consider withholding treatment?" he asked.

The renal fellow shrugged his shoulders. "No, frankly, nobody mentioned that." His deep voice became deeper. "The BUN was very high, 149, and the potassium was above 7 with EKG changes. All the studies demonstrated that treatment was indicated. Is Dr. Phillips suggesting that we withdraw the patient from hemodialysis?"

Phillips asked what the family thought.

"Family? They are all dead. She has a great nephew in Peoria, but we couldn't reach him. The social worker thought that he might be in a nursing home."

Ferguson, clearly chagrined, had selected this case to discuss management of electrolyte imbalance and fluid overload in post-op acute renal failure, not philosophy. He quickly asked Dr. Phillips what he thought of the rapid acid build-up. While it was interesting, the chief felt that it was irrelevant and asked what real benefit of treatment the team had expected.

Ferguson's face reddened, and his lips tightened. He pulled out a stack of lab reports pointing out that, according to these results, the situation was significantly improved. The chief could look at the reports himself.

In thirty years the chief had looked at enough reports; he again turned toward the head of the bed. The only movements under the sheets paralleled the bellows of the respirator and the pumping of the aortic balloon. He tried again to see the patient's face.

"Dr. Wilson," he asked as he looked at the name tag on the chest in front of him, "if this patient were your mother, eh, your great grandmother, would you want her to continue dialysis?"

Wilson, with all due respect, thought that she would rely on the opinion of the specialists. "The surgeon, the cardiologist and the pulmonologist all thought that treatment would improve her clinical condition."

"The specialists? Did you notice that each one is just looking at his own organ?" Phillips asked. The student blushed. "The heart is stronger, the lungs are improved, the infection is under control and the blood chemistries are better. But the patient seems about as full of life as an old vinyl garment bag."

The professor, who seemed disinterested in the BUN or potassium, wanted to discuss judgment, compassion and quality of life in this high tech age; but suddenly the ventilator alarm blasted, the cardiac monitor clamored and a large red stain spread across the sheet.

Bodies were flying, and books and clipboards went sailing into the air. Dr. Phillips ran to the head of the bed as the bulk of students darted out of the cubicle to make room for the inevitable, sweaty, foul-mouthed cardiac arrest team.

As Phillips ripped the sheet back, his head jolted forward, and his eyes leaped from his face. Ferguson's jaw fell, and he turned white and sweaty.

The bed was empty. Empty.

"Donna, get in here!" Phillips called to the head nurse. "What the hell is going on in here?"

The chief, with more than thirty years of clinical experience, had seen almost every conceivable problem; but this was the first patient problem where there was no patient.

Everyone who had remained in the room agreed; there was no body in that bed. The mattress was littered with a series of balloons, tubes, bottles and jars. A bag of blood had burst. The breathing tube led into a plastic bag from the Shop-Quick Market. The pulsating aortic balloon was jammed into a squeaking, bouncing Elmer's Dairy Barn mayonnaise jar. The large economy size. A piece of paper was taped to the jar.

"Donna," Phillips called again. But the head nurse always left the floor during renal rounds.

Ferguson looked at the reports and printouts. He could not explain the disappearance. According to his records, Agnes Mulligan was still there. The laboratory reports kept coming.

"Perhaps they came out of the bag of blood that burst," Phillips suggested.

"We had no problem with today's treatment," Ferguson added, as he wiped his face and nose with a yellow handkerchief. "The patient must have left after dialysis."

The professor wanted to know if she departed on roller skates or flew out the window.

Although he could not answer that question, Ferguson did not think that this was a complication of dialysis. "Just look at these lab reports." And there were no windows.

The nurses who were unable to escape were called into the room.

Mrs. Mulligan had been there for morning bath but weighed only 57 pounds, and it would be pretty easy to sneak her out of the hospital. She could have traveled in a small suitcase or duffel bag.

"I've always enjoyed renal rounds," a wide-eyed resident mentioned to Dr. Phillips as he walked across the room, "but today's
was the best."

The chief appreciated the praise.

Was Dr. Phillips going to write the case up?

The professor didn't think that it would be necessary. He was
sure that the Garfield Herald Examiner would take care of that.

Inquiries over the next few hours were not helpful. Phillips was
certain that the patient had been present for dialysis. To the best
of his knowledge, no one had ever reported adequate dialysis of a
mayonnaise jar.

"Why wasn't anyone aware of her absence before or during
rounds?" Dennis Lipsink, the hospital president wondered, shaking his head. But he was just an M.B.A. and did not understand
that no one was going to check the patient if all the monitors, con-
trols and alarms were okay. "And why this patient when we have
97% occupancy?"

Was he upset at having a profitable client stolen?

"Why wasn't security aware of the theft?" Lipsink asked.

The chief of security, brought into the inquisition, indicated
that they focused on people who come into the hospital and not
those who leave. Especially if they leave in a suitcase or shopping
bag.

President Lipsink thought that it might have been a kidnap-
ping.

Phillips felt that this was unlikely. Old Ms. Mulligan couldn't
command much of a ransom any more.

"Why did the thief go to the trouble of setting up a mechanical replacement?"

No one knew the answer to that question. No one had any idea until Phillips, absent-mindedly, looked at the wrinkled note on the back of the mayonnaise jar.

HASN'T AGNES ELSPETH MULLIGAN SUFFERED ENOUGH? DOCTORS – PLEASE – THERE IS A TIME TO LIVE AND A TIME TO DIE

From O.M.

An old First World War Vet

(1) Actually Cleveland was in his second presidential term

JUST A LITTLE PIECE OF PAPER

Do you have a living will and do you know where it is?

The lights flickered. Jennifer, lips moist and shiny, turned toward Bruce Hardenfast and smiled.

"No! No! Don't do it!" Adele Glassman cried. "Don't do it!"

It was too late. Jennifer's breast rose in her filmy red dress with the white lace trim as she leaned forward and pressed her cheek against Bruce's chest.

"Do you think," Adele asked, shifting her eyes from the T.V. to Murray, "that Judge Bennington will find out that Hardenfast is really Gretchen's father?"

"I hope so," Murray replied flatly.

"You do? Why?"

Murray confessed that he didn't really know why. "To tell the truth I wasn't paying much attention to 'Life's Little Headaches'."

"We're watching 'Quest for Undeniable Fulfillment.' "

"Sorry. I get them mixed up. Besides, I'm doing something more important. I'm filling out my living will, and I have one for you, too."

"Our will is all filled out, Murray. It's in the vault. Myrna and Alice get everything except for my gold earrings with the diamond droplet. I promised them to my cousin Blanche. It's settled."

"I'm not talking about that. This is a LIVING will. Be quiet for one minute and listen." Murray pushed his glasses up his nose and lifted a slip of paper from his lap. "When I, Murray A. Glassman, can no longer take part in the decisions for my future, let this statement stand as an expression of ......"

"You never could take part in the decisions for your future," Adele interrupted, "or we'd still have that lovely delicatessen on Taggett Avenue next to Milton's pet shop."

"Right, and I'd still have that stomach ulcer," Murray rebutted. "...stand as an expression of my wishes, while I am of sound mind," he shouted and waited for editorial comments about the soundness of his mind.

Adele, putting down the ball of wool she had been rolling, stood and turned off the TV. "Isn't a nice little ulcer better than standing behind the counter twelve hours a day for fourteen dollars and twenty-five cents an hour?"

"Shh. I'm not finished. If it should arise," Murray read quickly, "that there is no reasonable expectation of my recovery from physical and mental disability, I request that I be allowed to die and not....."

"What are you talking about? Why wouldn't I let you die? Did I ever stand in your way?" Adele sat down next to Murray and ran her fingers through the remnants of his graying hair.

"...and not be kept alive by artificial means or heroic measures."

Adele knew about heroic measures. She watched 'Society Hospital' at nine every Thursday on Channel Eight.

"What does reasonable expectation mean?"

Murray smiled. Adele was actually listening. "I'm not exactly sure, darling, but the doctors will know."

"Not Dr. Millington Branson. He wouldn't know. He's an alcoholic…and a brutal bloodthirsty rapist. Twice."

"But he's just a doctor in 'Society Hospital,' " Murray noted.

"So? What's so different between the soap operas and real life? Shouldn't we talk to the girls about this?"

"Okay, talk. But there is nothing to talk about. What this card says is that I don't want them to keep me alive if I will get no more pleasure from life and if I will only be a burden. I would rather be dead than a pomegranate."

"And what's wrong with pomegranates? Why are you doing this? Are you sick?"

"No. I'm as sound as a dollar. But we had a speaker at the club on Thursday. An ethical doctor. He said that if you didn't want them to shove a tube down your throat and pound on your chest when you're kicking the bucket, that you better fill out the white card and keep if with you."

"And if you fill out the card, then they won't do those things to you?"

"Maybe yes. Maybe no. The card isn't exactly legal in Pennsylvania. But it will give the doctors an idea of your wishes, and that might mean something when the time comes," Murray said. "Who knows? I started thinking about this stuff when they found that white spot on my chest x-ray last year."

"That was your Star of David twisted on the back of your shoulder."

"I know, but it made me think. I'm signing the card." And he scrawled Murray A. Glassman across the dotted line between 'signed' and 'this date' and shoved it in his wallet. He had to go to bed. Tomorrow was his twelve-hour day.

It was 10 P.M. Murray took off his apron and threw it on the counter. His feet hurt; he had a headache and wondered, as he locked the front door of the Fabulous Fifth Street Deli, if an ulcer could be worse than this.

Outside, the air was cold; it was raining and he turned his coat collar up. Then, as he neared his car, it happened fast. Someone or something tall ran out of the alley between the abandoned drug store and Pomerantz's Discount Hardware. Murray turned as an arm reached across his chest and pulled him down. When he hit the ground, it felt as if a rock had dropped onto the back of his skull. He rolled on the sidewalk and reached for his head. His hand was wet and sticky, and everything became fuzzy.

In what seemed like a moment later, he opened his eyes and looked up. Two bright lights made him squint, and Adele was smiling between the lights.

"What is she doing on Fifth Street?" Murray thought, and he was going to say that, but he could not talk. And his throat hurt like hell. He tried to swallow but could only retch.

"It's okay. Don't try to talk," Adele advised. "You have a tube down your throat."

Murray turned his head. That hurt too.

"This is Dr. Stetson. He saved your life, and all his little friends in green pants helped."

Murray didn't think his life needed saving, but his wife would never lie to him. The man standing next to Adele was short, skinny, pimple-faced and wore a white coat with red stains and bulging pockets. "Is he a counterman?" Murray wondered. "Where is his apron?"

"Thought we were going to lose you. But, don't worry; now you're going to be all right," the pimply guy said. "Since you are awake and alert, we should have you off the respirator in a day. Your lung is fully expanded, and the chest tube is clamped and should be coming out soon."

The words came fast and didn't make sense. Murray reached for this head with the arm that wasn't tied down and loaded with needles and tubes.

"Don't TOUCH that dressing." The doctor grabbed Murray's wrist. "There is a drain inside the bandage," Stetson explained. "It's draining the blood that pressed on your brain under the skull fracture."

Murray's vision was less blurred now, and he saw that tears were running down Adele's chubby cheeks. Her eyes were red, the lids puffy, and her hair was pulled back so that the gray roots showed. She wasn't wearing lipstick.

The little doctor thought that Murray would be able to leave the intensive care unit in forty-eight or seventy-two hours if he continued to make progress and kept his fat fingers off the dressing. "I'll be back a little later," he said and slipped out of the cubicle through the paisley curtain.

"He's single," Adele said. "Too bad he's not Jewish and has pimples." She walked around the bed and held Murray's free hand. "Oh, thank God that you're alive and with your family."

Murray tried to shake his head in agreement; but it hurt and, furthermore, where in the world was he, and where had he parked the car? He turned his head a bit and saw two women in the corner next to a sink. Except that one wore a jacket, they looked like the same person. Short, black hair, wide bottoms and round pale faces. Both were smiling and crying. It was Myrna and Alice.

"Give him some paper," Myrna or Alice said. "He wants to say something."

"Where the hell am I?" he wrote on a pad that said:

The Wharton Fels Maxwell Memorial Hospital
A Century of Care and Concern

And at the bottom of the sheet:

Practicing Today's Medicine Today

"You're in Maxwell Hospital on Baywood Avenue," Adele answered. "The police found you in an alley and brought you here. Your nose was in the mud. Your clothes were torn to shreds. You were practically dead. They couldn't identify you 'til a nurse thought you looked like the guy who had sold her potato salad and a half-pound of pastrami, sliced thin. For two days we didn't know where you were. I was going to jump off the roof and kill myself."

Should he feel guilty?

"He stole your watch and your wallet," Adele continued. "And your checkbook and credit card. He even took your Star of David, the bastard, and left you lying like a rat."

"Did they catch the guy?" Murray wrote.

"No. The son-of-a-bitch, he should burn in hell like Uncle Louie. They have no clues."

"Or maybe he should work at the Fifth Street Deli," Murray thought.

"Two minutes later and you would have been dead," Myrna said, or was it Alice? "You had a cardiac arrest just as they got you to the emergency room. Your ambulance was caught in traffic from the basketball game. Triple overtime. And you stopped breathing.

They worked on you for forty-seven minutes and eighteen seconds before your heart started working again. The doctors almost gave up, the nurse told me."

"It was the second longest resuscitation of the year," Alice said. "The little doctor won twenty-five dollars and a six-month subscription to 'Annals of Disaster Medicine.' "

"Then they thought you would be a vegetable," Myrna added. "You were out cold for nine days, Daddy."

His longest vacation in fourteen years, as a pomegranate.

"Why did they save me?" he wrote.

"That's their job. Didn't you want to be saved? You always said that you wanted to be around to play with your grandchildren."

Sure, but first the twins would have to meet some normal guys and get married.

Murray tried to shake his head, but it still hurt. Yes, he did want to be saved. Of course he is happy to be alive and with his family. "But what about my LIVING WILL?" he scribbled.

Alice shrugged her shoulders. She didn't know what that meant. "You must still be confused."

"You have a living will, Daddy?" Myrna asked. "I didn't know that. You never said anything, and the doctors didn't find one. You had no identification. You were Johnny Doe when they worked on you. Thank God they didn't find a living will."

"C'est la vie," Adele said and kissed her husband. Murray wondered which soap opera was in French.

It was pouring. The ambulance, lights flashing and siren blaring, followed by a blue and white police car, raced down Baywood Avenue, turned sharply at the iron gates and stopped in front of the emergency room next to seven other ambulances and the Villa de Roma pizza truck.

"This jerk was hit by a car while running across Clinton Avenue," the ambulance crewman explained. He pushed the stretcher through the crowd into trauma cubicle nine and helped lift the limp body onto the table.

"Where's the coffee?" a policeman asked.

"Hey, this guy is NOT breathing," a doctor shouted and pounded on the guy's chest. "Get anesthesia down here."

"They are down here, somewhere."

Three or four more people, in white jackets and green pajamas ran into the room and surrounded the blue body on the table, avoiding the wet, twisted leg that hung over the edge of the stretcher.

"Watch out, he's falling."

"This is the ninth damn code today, and I haven't had lunch."

"Get that E.K.G. hooked up and the lines in."

"Shit, I'm not getting a pulse."

"It's a straight line," someone else shouted. "Give me the Epi." The nurse handed him a syringe with a long needle, and he jabbed it into the chest after his jacket and shirt were ripped off.

At the same time two chattering women with green dresses, flowered cotton caps and red tackle boxes dashed into the room and toward the head that hung over the edge of the table.

"Bring his shoulders up," one of them said as she pushed a red pipe into his swollen mouth. "I think I'm in. You can hook him up."

"It's fibrillation," a doctor called out as he straddled the patient's abdomen and pushed on his chest. "Let's shock the son-of-a-bitch."

The patient's chest was squirted with jelly, and two silver paddles were pressed against the gray goop.

"Okay, zap him."

"Just wait a minute." The doctor on the table leaped off as he hit his head against an I.V. bottle. Everyone pulled back and pressed against the walls. Someone in the back of the room, probably the policeman, pushed a red button; and the patient's chest and head jumped up and fell back.

"Shit! Straight line. Gimme more Epi."

"And some calcium and bicarb and dopamine and…."

"Right. And Isuprel and neo."

"And lido."

"No lido, jerk-off!"

Another needle was jabbed into the chest, followed by a few quick injections into a tube under the collarbone.

"Fib," someone shouted.

Some more jelly and another squeeze on the paddles. The body jumped. A bit of gray smoke drifted up to the ceiling and set off the smoke detector.

"Looks like sinus rhythm."

"I'm getting a pulse," a deep voice in the crowd shouted.

"You can stop pushing, fatso," the policeman yelled.

Everyone applauded, shouted, hugged and ran out of the room. Only one red-headed woman and a tall skinny guy in a torn scrub suit with a pink lump on the right leg remained.

"Hey, where's the coffee?" the policeman asked again as the crew filed out.

"Ginny, let's get this mess cleaned up and see what we've got," the skinny guy, hands on hips, said from the back of the cubicle. The lump on his pants slid down onto his sneaker. The embroidered letters over his shirt pocket spelled: LL Endright, MD. Internal Medicine.

"Right, Larry," Ginny replied. "I think we're okay. His pressure is one ten over seventy, and he's regular." She dragged the patient's pants off and patted them until she pulled a wallet out of a slightly torn pocket.

Ginny called out from the cubicle and handed the wallet to a frowning guy in a blue shirt who poked his head through the curtains.

"Find out who this lox is, Marvin, and get in touch with the family."

A few minutes later Marvin, still frowning, was back at the table.

"Well?" Ginny asked.

"Murray Glassman."

"Glassman?" Ginny repeated. "Are you sure? This guy isn't even circumcised."

"Murray A. Glassman. 235 Troy Avenue. Apartment 4-B. I called his number."

"And?" Ginny asked.

""And no one answered," Marvin said.

"Maybe you dialed the wrong number. Call again."

"Look, I'm kinda busy. There's another code and two motorcycle accidents. I'll call later."

Marvin left and pulled the curtain shut. In a minute, he was back. "Oh, I forgot to tell you. I found a living will in his wallet. He don't want to be resuscitated if he kicks the bucket." Marvin held a little card in front of Ginny's face and then waved it at Endright. "See ya."

"He still has a pressure but isn't moving," Endright said. "And his pupils are unequal and don't respond to light. It looks like Murray's got some soft tissue damage, too, and a broken hip."

"Sounds like we won't have to order the dinner special for Mr. Glassman."

"Right. We'd better call neurosurgery and get a CAT scan right away. He's young. I think we can bring him around."

As Ginny turned to pull the pillow out from under the patient's neck and adjust the endotracheal tube, pink froth bubbled out from around the tube and the red light on the box above the bed started to flash and beep. The E.K.G. squiggles stretched out and flattened until a straight yellow line dashed across the screen followed by high pitched blasts from the box. The room refilled with the same friendly people who had greeted the patient earlier.

Endright jumped onto the table, whistled and held his arms out, palms up, as though he was stopping traffic. "Hold on, everyone. No code. Living Will. "THIS GUY IS A NO-CODE."

"Swell."

"Thank God."

The crew, jabbering and chirping, turned and dashed out of the cubicle.

"That's great," someone shouted as he ran out. "There's enough action without him. Let's get moving."

Now Ginny and Endright were alone again, except for the body with the straight line and no blood pressure.

"I'll pronounce him later," Endright said and followed the crowd down the hall.

Ginny shook her fist at Endright and turned to the body. She disconnected the endotracheal tube from the ventilator, untapped it and pulled it out of the patient's drooping purple mouth. "So young," she whispered.

As she pulled the sheet up to the dead man's neck and kicked an assortment of paper, bottles and bags into the corner, the curtain opened.

Marvin poked his head in and smiled. "I called Murray's number again, and this time his wife answered."

"Mrs. Glassman?"

"Yeah, I told her that her husband was in the Maxwell emergency room and wasn't doing too well. I didn't say that he was already dead."

"Good," Ginny said. "Is she coming in?"

"I think so. But Mrs. Glassman told me that it sounded funny because she had just left her husband. He was in room 218 and doing great. All his stitches were removed, and he could blow the yellow breathing ball all the way to the third column."

"The third column. That's weird," Ginny squinted.

"Mrs. Glassman told me that Murray was supposed to go home tomorrow. It didn't make any sense to her, but she's coming right over, anyway. Just to be sure. After she calls her lovely daughters."

Ginny shook her head. "Sounds bad, baby. I think we stepped in it this time."

Marvin didn't think so. He couldn't smell a thing.

Ginny pulled the curtain tight and started kicking the trash on the floor around again. Tears rolled down her cheeks and formed crooked dark streaks between her eyes and mouth.

The curtain rattled and when Ginny looked up, Endright was standing next to a short plump lady. They walked up to the table, and the woman leaned forward and took off her glasses. There were two shorter women behind her.

"He, eh, had a living will, Mrs. Glassman, so we didn't try to revive him," Ginny stammered and wiped her eyes.

"That's nice, darling, but this isn't my Murray."

The nurse turned away. Little beads of sweat popped out on her nose and upper lip.

"Well, I guess that this must be another Murray A. Glassman," Endright volunteered.

Adele shrugged. "It isn't my Murray."

It didn't seem to be the Murray of the ladies behind Adele, either. They were chatting and smiling.

Ginny pulled a gauze pad out of her pocket and blew her nose. She asked Marvin to call the Two South Nurses Station.

The ladies were right. The body wasn't their Murray. Their Murray was having Swiss steak with mashed potatoes and cauliflower.

Adele thanked everyone for letting this purple bloated stranger die…in peace.

"You are all so lovely, like television stars. Is the young doctor married?" she asked.

"No," the young doctor responded, "but I'm engaged to that nurse with the big breasts and red hair. The one with the dirty face. She's a critical care nurse."

"That's nice, darling."

Adele Glassman and her daughters smiled and turned toward the hallway. "Good-bye and stay well."

Before they went up to Two South, Doctor Endright wanted to ask the ladies a few questions.

"I've been up working for thirty-six hours, and I'm a little punchy. Do you folks live at 235 Troy Street?"

"For thirty five years," Adele answered. "Apartment 4-B. At one time it was quite a neighborhood. Doctor, maybe you have a brother?"

No brothers. Endright had two sisters and Twisty, a cocker spaniel. "Now I know that he's not your husband; do you know who this dead man is?"

"It's too late to save him now, isn't it, Doctor?" Adele responded.

"Yes, he's cold and quite stiff."

"In that case, we know him," Adele said. The twins shook their heads. "We've never seen him before, and we don't know his name, but we are pretty sure that he was not a nice guy."

"And I don't think he could read very well," Alice added.

Adele's eyes gleamed. "But, c'est la vie."

HIGHSTICK AND THE PROFESSOR

"Fifty cents a chance; four dollars a book," Freddie shouted. He was flat on his back. "Win a shiny ten-speed bike. Red with yellow stripes. Just half a buck."

Linda shook his shoulder. "Wake up, Fred. You're dreaming, and you're screaming. Everyone on the beach is staring. Wake the hell up."

The balding, somewhat stuporous man wiggled his head, wiped his eyes and sat up. His lumpy belly hung over his lime green bathing trunks. White sand trickled between his toes. He had no chances, and there was no bicycle.

"I thought I was on High Street, Lindy, in a raffle at the Knights Hall," he explained to his wife, sitting on a blanket in sunny Montego Bay.

"It was fun. I had a ball, felt very important and made two hundred bucks."

"That's nice, dear. That should pay for one of your shirts," his sun-tanned companion with long shiny red nails responded.

"No, darling, the money was for the Carol Yourchevsky Kidney Fund," he corrected in a husky voice clouded with mucous. "We need that money to pay for the dialysis machine for her home treatments. Her mother and Aunt Grace are training to do them. You met Carol. And the Knights of Columbus was having a dance, and the kids in the neighborhood were going door to door."

"That was thirty years ago. You haven't trained anyone for home dialysis in twenty years, and you haven't needed to raise a dime since the government started to pay for everything," Linda reminded him.

Now Fat Freddie Highstick was more awake and didn't need to be reminded that federal reimbursement had made him richer than he had ever dreamed.

"You were never home then," Linda pointed out. Somewhere under that bronze body was a remnant of the sweet young thing he married when he was an equally trim medical resident at the Garfield University Hospital. They called him 'the Stick' then.

"The kids grew up without knowing who their father was," she continued.

Fred shook his chins. He also wondered who their father might be as he settled back onto the blanket. Linda was discussing Gail Hamper's Olympic-size, Dutch tiled, heated indoor swimming pool and the fourteen-room addition to Gail's house in Butler Summit when her penetrating voice faded and fused with the breaking waves and calypso music drifting from the bar. His eyes closed, and he was back in Garfield City.

"So you want to go into nephrology, Dr. Highstick. Why, Frederick, would you want to do such a foolish thing?" Dr. Charlie Lancaster, Director of Nephrology at Mid-Atlantic Medical Center, asked.

Lancaster, rest his soul, looked like a genius but could ask the stupidest questions.

"Because the kidneys are fabulous organs, sir. I love them. They arc sophisticated and control the body's chemistry."

"That's nice, Fred, but if you go into the specialty, you'll be taking care of people whose kidneys don't work. Your focus will be on artificial kidneys and not on real ones."

"I know that, sir, but I plan on staying in academic medicine. Teaching and research. It makes more sense to try to prevent kidneys from failing than to replace their function with clunky machines."

Fred waited for the director to answer. In this highly competitive program, the Stick thought that he had just scored a few points, but Lancaster didn't answer. Instead, Linda slapped him on the face.

"If you're going to keep babbling, go back to the room," she suggested. "People will think you're on drugs." Apparently, he would get no credit for that fellowship interview.

Highstick sat up and rubbed his eyes. Why had she done that? And where was old Chuck Lancaster? Had he been dreaming again? The old director had died climbing a mountain when Highstick was still a full-time instructor at Mid-Atlantic. He was in the dog lab working on his acute renal failure prevention study when Betty, Lancaster's secretary, gave him the news. It was a shock. Even the dog seemed to take it badly.

"I guess that lying around in the sun made me think of the old days. The good old days, Linda."

Linda wondered what the good parts were. Was it a two-bedroom apartment with two little kids and the third on the way? Was it patching old clothes until they fell apart in your hands? Was it waking up in the middle of the night with the telephone ringing? Or was it waiting for Fred to come home after unclogging dialysis tubing or trying to wangle a new machine out of a ladies knitting club or the Sharpsfield Businessmen's Association?

No, Freddie thought that it was feeling that he was doing something for someone else, not just himself. Now that seemed a long time back. Only a dream.

"Before there were out-patient treatment facilities, you always worried about some helpless soul who needed dialysis but didn't have room for a machine at home or someone to help with the treatments," she reminded him. "How about the machine you had draining out the window into an alley because the patient didn't have plumbing? Fun. Some nights you couldn't eat your dinner you were having so much fun."

Well, he hadn't missed too many meals lately. Fred didn't have to worry about his poor homeless souls or drug addicts or his dear old folks, anymore. He had ninety-two kidney machines in six facilities with enough space and equipment to dialyze every patient in the three-county area who was unlucky enough to get kidney failure.

"So now I worry about the competition or the government."

"Yes. But now you can worry from Jamaica or the Zugspitze and not from a shack on Butler Street," Linda rebutted.

"Maybe I should have stayed in the lab instead of taking over that puny little hospital dialysis unit when Lancaster died."

"Right, Fred, and you'd still be wearing that worn out brown sport coat and skinny green tie," Linda reminded him.

"But it became a roller coaster ride after that. First the expanded unit, then transplants, then private practice and commercial facilities with stock holders, then ancillary services, then….."

The next 'then' was interrupted by a tan, uniformed young man seeking the where-abouts of one Dr. Frederick Highstick.

The Stick, after some wifely poking, revealed his hiding place and was escorted to a telephone, where someone at the other end seemed both far away and unhappy.

"Did you read this month's "Blue Journal of Medicine", Fred?" the voice asked. "Lead article."

"No. I don't think they have any copies at the Golden Crest Hotel."

"Well, it's big trouble," the voice warned.

"Who is this?"

"It's Jerry. Jerry Finletter."

The Stick, standing in the beachfront bar in sandals and a mini-robe, had trouble putting the name in the right slot.

"Ken Stuhlbreaker, at Eastern Ohio, just published a study on reversing the progression of renal disease. Twelve hundred white JLT mice and no loss of kidney function."

"So what, Jer. I have nothing against JTL mice." Freddie had just found a slot for Finletter. He was a nephrologist. Wasn't every one? And he owned twelve dialysis units scattered throughout Kentucky. He did some TV ads. Used a dog and a guy who had been a cowboy star when they still kissed their horse. And Finletter was vice-president of the National Dialysis Physicians Association. Fred was on the board.

"So what!" Finletter repeated. "I don't know about you, but I'm heavily financed in my units. I can't handle some jerk cutting down the flow of patients. Man, those advertising fees are going out the window."

The Stick had his problems too. Personnel costs were up, and he needed capital for his new ventures. There was the low choles-terol farm and the paraffin bath franchises. And was he going to invest in the "Golden Years Home Cancer Detection Kit"?

"Whatta you want me to do, Jerry?" The Stick asked. "Is the asso-ciation going to meet on this?"

"No. The damn guys are too slow. They had a chance to stop it two years ago before it got out of hand. I think just a few of us should deal with this," Finletter advised.

Apparently, Fred was one of the few. He would head home as soon as he could get a flight.

Headquarters of the National Dialysis Physicians Association was wherever its president lived. Fat Freddie got the next plane to Miami, then a flight to Detroit and finally a taxi to a marble and glass living room, eighty-seven dollars north of the airport.

"You look great in straw shoes, Highstick," Harriet Genzler bellowed as Fred walked into that living room. "Have a seat."

Gentzler, a.k.a. Hotcakes, didn't make it sound as though he had an option, and he fell into a plush suede chair.

Hotcakes was from his generation, and, although she had trained in Chicago, they traveled in the same circles. While among the top ten dialysis breadwinners and president of the kidney capitalists club, she was, above all else, recognized as the nephrologist with the biggest balls. Twenty-two board certified physicians with lesser gonadal tissue worked for her.

"Fred, say "hello" to Jerry Finletter and Bruce Crawley."

He did. Fred had last seen Kentucky Jerry at the international meeting in Monte Carlo. Crawley, who had flown in from L.A., was hidden behind dark glasses, half swallowed by a suede chair. Highstick could not place him. But if he always wore glasses with thick red and silver frames, and if he always twitched rhythmically, recognition would not be a problem in the future.

After giving his drink order to someone who, clearly, was not a board member, Hotcakes filled Freddie in on the chitchat.

"This is what we call damage control," she began. "The perception is that old Stuhlbreaker will have a cure for kidney failure in eighteen to twenty-four months. Even if he is off base, his research has hit the web sites; and the big investors believe that the flow of new patients will dry up within three years."

"Three years?! In science it's hard to be precise. But in business they know everything," Finletter added.

"This isn't science, Jerry, and it's not even clinical medicine. This is industry," Gentzler added quickly. "At this point it doesn't matter if Stuhlbreaker can't cure heat stroke in Alaska, the big money will think he's got the cure."

"So you're saying that we've got to change that impression in the minds of the big investors," Crawley echoed from deep within his cushion.

"Right."

"How?" Fred asked.

"Our money men can't see this guy as the savior of end-stage kidney disease patients," the president replied.

"What do we know about Stuhlbreaker?" Fred asked.

"More than we need to, but what difference would it make if he had green hair and horns?" Gentzler rebutted. "Would it matter if he was six foot nine and batted right and threw left?"

Freddie, finger in the air, was preparing an answer. Fortunately, his drink came. He took a sip and silently offered thanks that he wasn't one of Genzler's Detroit crew.

In the real world Kenneth L. Stuhlbreaker, M.D., PhD, was Professor of Medicine and Physiology at the Warren G. Harding College of Medicine in Akron, Ohio and had been there for twenty-two years. Although he had worked diligently in his lab since the day of his appointment, no one in Gentzler's living room, including Nelson the butler, could recall any major achievements of the aging professor. Unless you counted the Stuhlbreaker pipette, used to suck the juice out of guinea pig pituitary glands. Or unless you considered his ability to get grant money from the federal government.

"Well, I guess it doesn't matter what the research is about, either," Freddie conceded.

"Now you're getting it," Gentzler replied.

Actually, the project was quite clever. Stuhlbreaker was working with a new chemical agent that lowered the pressure in glomeruli, those millions of cute little filters in the kidney. When the pressure was lowered, the little mice's tiny kidneys weren't damaged. The journal article noted that the agent worked no matter what diabolical means was used to injure those cute little rodent organs. His were the happiest mice in America.

"Okay, but how do we discredit the little professor or stop his work?" Finletter asked. "And how do we do it quickly?"

"Just a minute, guys," the Stick cautioned. "If this is legitimate stuff and will keep people off dialysis, should we be doing this? What about the Hippocratic oath?"

Crawley had heard something about that oath, but couldn't remember what it was. (*)

Gentzler thought that preventing kidney failure was playing into the hands of a small interest group. "It certainly is not consistent with the highly technical direction of modern medicine and could undermine the entire health care system."

"In balancing the needs of a mere hundred thousand patients against the entire economy of the free world, we have got to come down on the side of stopping Stuhlbreaker," Finletter agreed.

The question was how to do it in a way that would satisfy Wall Street.

"We don't have enough time to review the work and shoot holes in it," Gentzler thought. "It's in a preliminary phase, and the most effective approach is to keep it from going any further. And for business to realize that it is dead in its tracks."

"How do we do that?" Highstick asked. "Do we shoot the guy?"

"Exactly what I was thinking," Gentzler agreed.

Suddenly something strange was happening in the living room. Total silence.

HIghstick leaned forward and shook his head slowly. The guests could not form words or emit sound. Finally, Crawley, some color returning to his face, pulled off his glasses and stared at the leader. "You are kidding."

No, she was not kidding.

The Stick rose to get out of his chair, but couldn't get enough lift in his flabby thighs and fell back.

"You want to shoot Stuhlbreaker?" Finletter asked.

"Do you think it's a bad idea?"

Three heads shook quite a bit. Apparently, they thought it was.

"I guess you are right," she conceded. "Too messy. Too easy to trace. We've got to think of a better way to kill him."

Highstick tried again and still couldn't get out of his chair.

"Look, when you guys agreed to serve the interest of the kidney docs, you assumed an obligation. How can you stack the life of some old twerp against that duty?" Genzler shouted as she rose and marched around the room. "And the way you've boxed yourselves in with your investments, if he lives, you are as good as dead."

"But we're not murderers," Freddie protested.

"Think about that," she quickly rebutted.

Finletter conceded that they might know a little about the subject.

"If we put our heads together", Gentzler thought, "we could come up with a procedure to eliminate their problem."

After several minutes of rapid drinking, Finletter had a thought. Gentlzer leaned over the bronze coffee table, head forward, elbows on thighs in an attentive pose. "My old high school teacher blew himself up in his chemistry lab. On his birthday."

"Great, Jerry," Freddie shot back. "How do we convince the professor to explode?"

"Actually, that is not a bad idea," Crawley declared. "I visited Warren Harding a few years ago and was in Stuhlbreaker's lab."

"Did he seem flammable?" Highstick asked.

"He certainly did," Crawley replied. "He smokes constantly and drops ashes everywhere. If there was anything combustible in the lab, he'd be gone."

"Fortunately for him the mice are fire resistant."

"That's it," Finletter screeched.

"That's it?" the others asked.

"Yes. We'll make his mice explosive, and he can kill himself," Finletter explained.

With that, Gentzler slapped Finletter on his shoulder and described the chemical properties of various ingredients in bug killers, ink eradicators and a few other charming household products. Chemicals such as methyl pyrrolidone and methyl carbamate.

"We can add it to the rodent feed and water. We'll have it poured into their cages, and they can roll in it. And for good measure we can add it to the water supply of the fire sprinkler system so that the room will be sprayed with explosives when the fire starts. The professor won't have a chance. And any evidence will be blown into the next county."

The committee members seemed impressed. After some discussion they agreed that it could be done without any of them going anywhere near the little lab.

Nine days later, large parts of the west wall of the Millard Fillmore Basic Science Building of the Warren Harding College of Medicine, Akron, Ohio were blown into the staff parking lot. Seven cars and the statue of an obscure American president sustained damage; but, fortunately, no one in the lot was killed or injured.

Within the building, however, it was estimated that four hundred white mice and one professor of medicine and physiology were killed. There were no other injuries.

That evening, the city watched the Fire Commissioner, the Chief of Police and the Vice-President of the Medical School on the Channel Ten eleven o'clock news.

"We assume that the few body parts that were recovered belonged to Professor Kenneth Stuhlbreaker," Police Chief Glitter answered, in response to a question from Anchorwoman Lynn Christiansen Gomez. "His laboratory was destroyed. He did not show up for dinner and the charred remains of his cigarette lighter were found in what was left of the room."

"How could this happen in a modern fire proof building?" the anchor wanted to know.

Fire Commissioner Burt Pularsky didn't know, but there will be a complete investigation. "Professor Stuhlbreaker was known to be a heavy smoker. We will start there."

Gomez asked the police chief if they suspected foul play.

Glitter tilted his head and squinted at the anchor without answering.

Gomez whirled quickly in her chair and faced the school V.P. "Doctor Becker, what effect will this have on the valuable research for which the professor was receiving world-wide attention?"

"Fortunately, Dr. Stuhlbreaker kept all his data in a fifth floor office," the vice-president noted. "That office seems to be on the fourth floor now, but the desk is intact, and the work can go on."

"Who will do it?" Ms. Gomez asked.

"I will," the V.P. responded quickly. "I was a nephrologist, a renal physiologist and a biochemist before I went into, uh, administration. I will do the work. We owe it to Dr. Stuhlbreaker's memory, to his wife and to the NIFI, the National Investigative Funding Institute."

The anchor understood.

Eight days after the nine days, the city that was saddened by the medical school tragedy was now shocked by its investigation.

Police Chief Glitter, on his way to stardom on the eleven o'clock news, announced that "Professor Stuhlbreaker did not blow himself up as had been assumed. The great researcher was murdered."

Gomez puckered her lips at the chief and shook her head quite slowly.

"We have substantial evidence," Glitter continued, "which indicates that the laboratory was peppered with explosives."

The anchor wanted to know who the murderer or murderers were. Now it was the chief's turn to smile.

"And why would anyone want to kill this benign and loveable old man?" the anchor asked. "Could it have something to do with his research?"

"Yes, indeed." Glitter thought that this was the first clue.

Clue two would have something to do with individuals who would be familiar with chemicals, explosives and that sort of stuff.

Those clues were pretty meager. The third clue was the best. It came from a very nice gentleman in Detroit who was the butler to a prominent physician.

The third clue, in fact, was great. Six days after the eight days, four senior nephrologists were taken into custody and charged with the murder of one Kenneth L. Stuhlbreaker, age sixty-six.

How did they plead?

"Not guilty."

A jury of five men and seven women disagreed.

Drs. Genzler, Finletter, Crawley and Highstick no longer needed to be concerned about investments, advertising costs, unfair competition or future risky business ventures. They had, at last, achieved security: secure ninety-nine year sentences without eligibility for parole.

In the final analysis, they saw their duty, and they did it. But had they really saved the world from a cure for kidney disease?

Good to his word, Vice-President Becker hung up his three-piece suits and designer ties and returned to the research lab. The Stuhl-breaker data and procedures seemed simple enough. Then, in an undamaged laboratory, he set out to duplicate the preliminary data. Many more mice would die. Had he spent too much time in the board-room and the clubs? All his mice died in florid kidney failure. The old professor's magic chemical didn't save one little mouse. Not one.

Christiansen Gomez, quite the pest, called every Thursday for a progress report. Becker pleaded for more time.

"The station is being flooded with letters," Gomez responded. "The professor and his work have become a cause. The public must be served."

Finally, after extensive review with many highly regarded scientists, and after recruitment of a small army of young and eager researchers, Becker was able to report his finding. He would do that on the eleven o'clock news.

"As was originally reported in the "Blue National Journal of Medicine" none of Stuhlbreakers mice progressed to renal failure," Becker noted. "The report concluded that the chemical EX 2341-B had prevented the renal disease from progressing."

A growing number of sweat beads dotted his forehead. "We now believe, however, that Dr. Stuhlbreaker, may he rest in peace, had not, in fact, created any kidney disease for EX 2341-B to reverse," Becker whispered.

"Does that mean that the chemical was not effective?" Gomez needed to know.

"Yes, it does", the vice-president acknowledged. "When actual renal failure was created, the EX 2341-B proved as effective as lemonade and tap water."

"Does that mean that there will be no change in the treatment of kidney failure patients in the foreseeable future, Doctor?"

"I'm afraid that it does, Ms. Gomez," Becker agreed. "Dr. Stuhlbreaker's studies have been terminated and will not be renewed."

That was very sad news, indeed. The following morning, after reading newspaper accounts in their cells, Drs. Highstick, Genzler, Finletter and Crawley would certainly agree.

(*) see below – Hippocratic Oath

BEN CLEARFIELD – LADY KILLER

"How about this one, guys," Ronnie Picker announced as he turned to page five. "Probe of City Streets Department completed: overtime declared excessive."

Lew Caulder's elbow rested on the table, and his chin sank into his hand. Larry Kline moaned, and Jack Green snored. Ben Clearfield's eyes closed, and his balding head bobbed slowly.

"Shut the hell up," Larry Kline demanded. "Who gives a damn about the streets department?"

"Then wait 'til you hear this one," Ron bellowed. "Prominent Garfield City attorney found guilty in the ax slaying of his voluptuous socialite wife."

Ben Clearfield opened his eyes, and the bodies round the table in Chuck's Pub stiffened.

"A jury of seven men, four women and one unidentifiable creature concluded, after four and a half minutes of deliberation, that Cedric Gainsworth had hired two unemployed meat packers to section his wife and discretely distribute her body parts in the city and surrounding areas."

"That guy must have hated to go home more than you, Bennie," Kline concluded. Ben Clearfield smiled and shook his head.

"The District Attorney had no trouble linking Gainsworth to the two...."

"Gainsworth must be the dumbest lawyer east of the Mississippi," Clearfield declared. "Anyone with half a brain can kill his wife and get away with it."

"And how would you do it?" Picker challenged.

Silence. Clearfield sipped his scotch and accepted the conclusion of his drinking buddies that he was nothing more than an old stock brokering bag of wind. And an ugly one.

"No axes for me," Clearfield thought as the wobbly middle-aged businessmen gathered their computer cases and cell phones and headed into the cool Garfield City air.

"No hacksaws, shotguns or howitzers," he thought as he walked to the Marshall Avenue Spice Shop. "No chains or explosives. A little pepper, vinegar and flavoring will do."

An hour later, the Butler Summit bus turned left onto 36th Street and discharged its only passenger. He hated the smelly bus, yet month after month, year after year, the damn ride seemed to get him home faster.

"How are the boys?" Vivian asked.

"Fine. Just fine, darling." Ben was trying to sound sober while wondering if Vivian really cared about the drinking buddies she had never met.

"What's for dinner?" he asked.

It was Friday. It was pepper steak.

"Pepper steak, Ben."

"Can your stomach handle it, Vivian?"

He was told that her stomach was just fine today. She had seen Dr. Stoker, and he gave her a prescription for cimetadine. He wasn't sure if it was her gallbladder, pancreas or duodenum, but she would be all right.

"Pancreas? How does he know that you have a pancreas? Did he order any tests?"

"No tests. Only if things don't get better."

When Vivian headed off to the kitchen, her concerned husband pulled a small bottle out of his jacket pocket and dropped a bit of white powder into her chicken soup.

When she returned, dinner proceeded with its usual precision and silence. Over the years, Ben's little lady quickly approached and then overran the two hundred pound hurdle. Was that why he hated her? They had stayed together through three failed businesses, two affairs and the westward migration of Roger, their only child. But why did he need to kill her now? And why, he wondered, did he wait until he was bald and impotent?

After Vivian lowered a bowl of pickled beets onto the table, she pulled a letter from her apron and handed it to Ben. It was from darling Roger, who had moved to northern Utah. He was in a religious retreat of holistic agrarian mineralopaths and would live only on pinecones and high-grade bituminous coal. Ben shoved the letter in his pocket and dinner continued.

As they cut, ripped and chewed their way through red and brown mounds of food, Vivian's expression became increasing pained. The meat, the potatoes and even the beets echoed within her and periodically tried to escape.

"Look how you are suffering, darling. It's been more than six weeks, and Dr. Stoker hasn't done a thing for you."

"I have good days and bad days."

That was true. Ben needed to decrease the number of good days.

"I think Stocker is too old-fashioned. Asher Kligman was telling me about a new G.I. doctor at Mid-Atlantic. His name is Thompson. Thompson Wainwright. A surgeon. Stocker was treating Kligman's wife for an ulcer for years. It turned out that what she had was a shoelace clogging her jejunum. Wainwright removed it, and her pain disappeared completely."

Vivian seemed a bit skeptical.

"From a high top sneaker."

"It usually starts at dinner, and it sometimes wakes me at night," Vivian explained as she pushed her fists into her solar plexus. "My doctor gave me medicines, but the pain and the gas kept getting worse. Ben, he's my husband, thought that I was using too much salt and seasoning, so now he does all the cooking." She paused long enough to burp for the new doctor. "My Benjamin is very worried about me. To be honest, I wouldn't be here if he hadn't insisted."

The doctor jabbed his right hand into the middle of her belly and lifted it quickly.

Dr. Wainwright was so young and good looking she thought. Why hadn't Roger stayed in school and become a handsome young doctor?

"We're going to have to run some tests, Mrs. Clearfield, endoscopy and an MRI. And, of course, lots of blood studies."

"Ben said you would."

"I think it is your gallbladder, and it will probably have to come out. Before that, however, I want to make sure that it isn't something I can't operate on. We wouldn't want that, would we? I mean, we wouldn't want to operate on you when it was not necessary."

Vivian smiled and fluttered her purple streaked eyelids. Wainwright could operate on her for any damn thing he wanted.

Two weeks later in the Suburban Community General Hospital Family Lounge and Salad Bar, Ben saw handsome young Wainwright walking toward him and thought that this would be a good time to start pacing up and down nervously.

"Good news, Mr. Clearfield. The gallbladder is out, and Vivian is doing fine. She'll be in recovery for about an hour, and then you can see her."

"Fortunately, Ben was prepared for the surgeon's "good news". Nothing had come easily in thirty years. Apparently, the gallbladder came out without a fight. (*) They sure don't make them the way they used to. None-the-less, he had to parlay that timid bag of bile into a real killing.

"The gallbladder didn't show many signs of inflammation, but you can't always tell by the gross appearance."

In the language of surgery that meant that the gallbladder was normal. If the concerned husband hadn't called the concerned surgeon every forty-eight hours to detail Vivian's cramps and eructations, that innocent little green sack would still be resting under her floppy liver.

"We anticipate an uncomplicated post-operative course, Mr. Clearfield."

They always do. But in a two hundred twenty pound endomorph lying in bed with a tube down her nose and into her stomach something just might go wrong. Ben's job was to see that it did or his months of planning and manipulation would be fruitless. After all, Vivian had many faults, but only one gallbladder.

Forty-eight hours later Benjamin J. Clearfield walked toward the nurses' station on the post-operative wing of 2 West. He looked worried. Ben was proud of that look.

"Miss Tinsley, my wife feels like she has a bit of fever; could you check her temperature?"

Of course Jennifer Tinsley would check the temperature. Mr. Clearfield needn't be concerned, however. "It isn't unusual for patients to have a bit of fever after a cholecystectomy. It's due to little collapsed areas in the lungs because of secretions and generally gets better on its own," she assured him. "We call that atelectasis," Nurse Tinsley indicated, as she removed the thermometer, "and that is why she should be using that breathing tube on her bedside table."

Loyal Ben shook his head.

"100.4. That's not very high. We'll give her two Tylenol tablets."

"Don't you think we had better call Dr. Wainwright?" he asked. "If pneumonia is setting in, I know that he will want to nip it in the bud."

Because the vigilant spouse seemed distressed, the doctor was called, and he wanted to give Vivian two Tylenol tablets and keep an eye on the temperature and be sure that she does her breathing exercises. No need for antibiotics.

Ben followed the low-grade fever attentively and reported his findings to the staff faithfully. Eventually, after a number of animated, and occasionally tearful, discussions of this febrile period, the doctor agreed with the stockbroker that a chest x-ray, perhaps followed by antibiotics, was not a bad idea.

The chest x-ray was normal. No pneumonia. No further treatment was necessary, but if antibiotics would decrease Mr. Clearfield's concern and his telephone calls, the doctor would happily order a nice little expensive semi-synthetic penicillin.

Ben certainly would not upset the surgeon by reminding him of Vivian's penicillin allergy. That trivial bit of information had been on a flimsy red sticker on the front of her chart until, with a bit of assistance, it lost its stickiness and fell, face down, onto the carpeting. Vivian was given the medication, and two days later her skin erupted into a bumpy purple pattern. One area looked like a relief map of New Zealand.

A shiny new sticker was pressed onto the chart. Three days later, Ben was able to report that the rash didn't seem to be getting better. And, my, did it itch.

"Now it has spread to the folds in her neck, Miss Tinsley."

The obviously worried husband pulled out his soggy handkerchief and blew his nose. Poor Ben was in tears again.

Nurse Tinsley explained that the antibiotic had been stopped and, therefore, the rash would certainly disappear. Eventually. "Perhaps the longer you look at it, the longer it will take." Ms. Tinsely seemed to be a firm believer in the "watched pot" theory.

Ben explained to her, and later to the surgeon, that he was especially worried because his uncle Lew had died of a purple rash after he was given penicillin for a small pimple on the back of his right ear.

"My friend, Jack, who does the books for a dermatologist in Patterson, said that if they had given Uncle Lew prednisone, he would be alive today."

"I understand your concern, sir, but prednisone is what we call a steroid," Dr. Wainwright explained slowly. "And while it may clear the rash faster, the medication can be very irritating to the stomach and cause ulcers with bleeding. We certainly don't want to take that risk."

"We certainly would not, but what about Uncle Lew? He was my favorite uncle. When I was a kid, he took me to the baseball game every Saturday. And he left a wife and three children." Ben sighed. "After all, Doctor, she is the only wife I've got."

Dr. Wainwright had, for some time, suspected that this was true. After two or three additional discussions about Uncle Lew and his grieving widow and his little daughters who had to give up piano lessons, Dr. Wainwright thought that a short course of prednisone might get Mrs. Clearfield, and her husband, out of the hospital faster.

The prednisone did its job. Given in full doses, it worked tirelessly on the itch, on the rash and on Vivian's stomach lining. She vomited dark grainy gruel. The next day, Mark Fortune, the hospital gastroenterologist, found a clean little crater on the back wall of her stomach with his little endoscope; and sure enough, it seemed to be bleeding. Dr. Fortune took some pictures of the crater and pasted them on the bloated chart.

"The stubborn ulcer kept bleeding," Dr. Wainwright explained to red-eyed Ben Clearfield, "and Vivian needs blood and is a rare blood type."

Ben knew that.

As they sat together, glumly, outside the surgical ICU, the doctor agreed that it probably wasn't a bad idea to call Roger and have him fly east from Utah.

"She is going to get better," the surgeon assured Ben, "but she certainly would be comforted by the sight of her dear son."

Ben thought that the surgeon didn't look as young as he had three weeks ago. In fact, he was starting to look a little bit like Roger. He was such an eager and suggestible chap, exactly what this case called for. Ben would remember to send him a Christmas card every year.

At that moment, the green door swung open, and the nurse who was working on Vivian's falling blood pressure and labored breathing called Wainwright into the ICU. That gave Ben time to decide how to establish contact with his son, the Herbal Priest. As he thumbed through his black book for the address of the Church of Natural Sunlight, the doctor returned, sat down and put his right hand on Ben's left shoulder. Ben had seen that gesture several times on <u>Thursday Night House Doctor</u>. It always occurred within the last four minutes of the episode.

"The good news, Mr. Clearfield, is that we stopped the prednisone and the bleeding has stopped," the surgeon related for openers.

Ben knew that it had, but not before Vivian developed shock and a seizure following a transfusion reaction. With that hand on his shoulder, Ben knew that his job was over. At this point, Wainwright and his crew could finish without him.

"However, she is still in shock; and it looks like she may have thrown a blood clot from her leg to her lung," the doctor continued. "It's probably due to prolonged bed rest in a large woman." Ben knew that, too. "We may have to operate on her this evening to prevent any further clots from dislodging."

Ben asked if Vivian was strong enough for the operation. As he signed the consent form, he really wanted to know if Wainwright was strong enough.

Two days later, Roger, in full headdress, geode beads and walrus moccasins sat on the floor next to his father, the white man.

"Oh, most holy parent, root of my being, giver of my gene pool, (**) what else can befall our most beloved woman?"

As the priest spoke, Dr. Wainwright approached. Ben looked at the healer's pale, down-turned face and knew instantly that nothing else would befall their most beloved woman.

"Ben, Roger. It looks like Vivian's suffering is over," the surgeon muttered. Roger did not understand. Had they found a new painkiller? Ben realized that, indeed, the best place for his son was in the hills of Utah eating smooth rocks.

"No, I'm afraid that your mother has passed."

Passed. Roger looked confused.

"Your mother has expired."

Roger's eyes opened wide. "You mean she is dead."

Ben knew that you had to go slowly with Roger. Three tries and he got it.

"Yes," the surgeon confessed. "I'm so sorry. I guess we never knew how sick she really was."

Ben knew how sick she really was. Two weeks before his first visit to the spice shop, she had picked up their piano and moved it into the dining room.

The priest fell to the floor. With his head bowed, tears rolled down his cheeks and wilted the feathers on his headdress.

His father, on the other hand, couldn't get any tears to roll. Perhaps his ducts had worn out. Ben knew that he better look mournful and concentrate on the right thing to say.

"Better luck next time, Doc."

Maybe that wasn't perfect, but it seemed to cheer Wainwright a bit.

"Same to you, Ben."

It was Friday night. Ron Picker rustled and shook the paper. The customary call for silence.

"How about this one. Page one. Long time Garfield City stockbroker wins record suit. Benjamin C. Clearfield awarded seven point three million dollars in the wrongful death of his rightful wife."

Below the story was a picture of the grieving widower, handkerchief in hand, leaving the courthouse with a man that Picker thought looked like a 19th Century Choptank Indian.

Picker waited for Ben to correct his syntax, as he always did. But, of course, Ben was not there. He was somewhere in the South Pacific. The widower was on a quiet tropical island with an herbal priest who had recently discovered that there were more enjoyable things to eat than petrified crustaceans.

As Roger shared his father's new home, he seemed to exude a sense of warmth and caring. "I am pleased to share your home and hearth, dearest father."

Ben wondered how many hearths there were in the South Seas.

"But, most beloved ancestor," Roger continued, "I am most concerned for your well-being. You seem distressed. As you sleep, I see you clutch at your stomach. And wondrous sounds rise from your bowels. Perhaps you need the care of a western healer, an American doctor."

The father assured his son that he would be all right. "I just have to adjust to the food down here," Ben explained. "I will be just fine."

Roger was not so sure. He would watch his father closely. He would see that he got all the care that he deserved. And Roger would do all the cooking.

(*)When this account was written, a cholecystectomy was an inpatient procedure.

(**) i.e. 50% of Roger's pool including the Y chromosome

DOING THE BEST WE CAN

Arthur took the cup from the cabinet, rinsed and dried it several times and set it on the center of the placemat. After sliding a tea bag into the cup and winding the string around the handle three times, he picked up the kettle with two potholders and poured the water.

Arthur Blankenship was a very careful man. He had courted Jeanette Forsythe for seven years before asking for her hand in a complex sentence with several modifying phrases and three disclaimers. Jeannette, guided by different instincts, answered before the question was completed. None-the-less, referring to his notes, Arthur completed the proposal as he had composed it.

Arthur's attention to detail was greatly valued at Garfield City Life and Casualty, where he had worked as an actuarial since graduating from Marshall College of Business and Commerce. Despite a record devoid of irregularities, incidents, absences or lateness, he had anticipated a negative response from Mr. Shumann, the office manager, when he asked for a leave of absence for surgery, which could no longer be delayed.

Mr. Schumann, however, approved the leave without hesitation. "I am pleased that you've decided to have the operation before complications set in." With frightening hospital stories in the newspapers almost every day, he understood Arthur's concern regarding hospitalization and surgery; but, after all, a hernia repair was a simple matter. Last month his nephew, Bruce, had two or three done as an outpatient during his lunch break.

Mr. Schumann took the opportunity, again, to remind Arthur that the hernia was probably the result of climbing up and down sixteen flights of stairs every day. Although the elevator had gotten stuck twice, six years ago, it had been thoroughly overhauled and had passed inspection every six months with no deficiencies. Thousands of normal passengers rode it daily.

Arthur, unconvinced, would continue to use the stairs, which were quite sturdy and not subject to mechanical breakdown.

"Are you going to have the operation at Suburban Community?" Mr. Schumann asked. "They tell me the food there is great."

"But what about the skill of the surgeons, the condition of the operating rooms, the surgical instruments and the training of the nurses? And what about the support services and the precision of the laboratory? There are many factors that should go into critical health care decisions."

"So where is it going to be?" Mr. Schumann asked. "Mid-Atlantic or that snooty Garfield University Hospital? They'll put you in a broom closet they call a semi-private room. And the TV reception is terrible. At Suburban Community they treat you like a king. They have a therapist just for back rubs. And a maître-d' and a wine steward."

"I'm not going to have the operation in Garfield City, sir," Arthur responded.

"Well, where are you going to go? Tokyo? Do you really want a foreign-made hernia repair?"

"No. It will be in this country. But I have not decided on the city, the hospital or the surgeon. I didn't want to rush it. I hope you understand."

"Okay, my boy, take your time. But remember, the crab bisque at Suburban is magnificent. Rich and creamy with big chunks of crab," Mr. Schumann advised as he walked from Arthur's cubicle.

That evening Arthur pulled a stack of computer printouts and reports from his file cabinet and spread them across the kitchen table. Jeanette was in bed, and he would have the solitude needed to make the final calculations. He had a vast body of statistics, both private and governmental, gathered over the years, that would allow him to determine the hospital with the fewest complications and the best surgeon.

At City Life and Casualty, the word at the coffee pot was that Arthur reviewed the Business Weekly and Consumer Guidepost before buying a box of raisins. It was not true. Arthur did not eat raisins; they get caught between your teeth and cause cavities. They could tease him about little things; but this hernia was getting bigger, and he wasn't going to make the same mistake as Gloria Tomicelli in Accounts Receivable. She had her gallbladder removed at Mid-Atlantic. But how did she know if it was really taken out? She didn't get a second opinion. Even worse, after surgery she got a clot in the long vein in her right leg and had to take blood thinners for a year. You could bleed to death from that. She hadn't, but she was lucky. That wasn't going to happen to him.

Arthur was reviewing the data when he sensed that he was not alone. Looking down, he saw a pair of floppy slippers with soft brown rabbit's ears on the floor next to his chair.

"Arthur, it's two o'clock. You have to go to work in the morning; please come upstairs," Jeanette pleaded.

He looked up and explained that he was in the middle of a critical calculation and was almost finished. "Furthermore, Jeanette, tomorrow is Saturday," Arthur pointed out as he patted the left ear of her right slipper.

"In the old days," he explained, "patients were kept in the dark. They had to rely on what their doctors told them. Medical care was simply based on confidence."

"I know," Jeanette responded, as she yawned. "We loved old Doctor Murphy, and we trusted him."

"But you had no way of knowing if he was right. Today we have reams of statistics that rate care. We know which surgeons have the lowest complication rate for every operation from removal of a wart to replacement of blood vessels and heart valves."

"Like a batting average." Jeanette seemed to be catching on.

"Right. And we have batting averages on the hospitals, too." He pointed to reports on which hospitals gave the most enemas to the wrong patient and the most mismatched blood transfusions. "Here are the figures on the cost of blood counts; here's one on the average length of stay after every illness based on age, sex and political party. This sheet lists the average hospital room temperature in March 2010."

"If you have the operation at Mid-Atlantic, Artie, I can walk over during lunch to visit you."

Arthur thought that was sweet but didn't fit into any formulas he had developed. "With these formulas I rated every hospital in the country and every board-certified general surgeon. By combining the two I have just chosen the doctor and the hospital. Look at this," he said, handing Jeanette a fourteen-pound printout. "This lists every hospital in the country from the best to the worst. Bolton Hospital in Bolton, Massachusetts is the best. Roosevelt Hospital in Danville, Colorado is second."

Jeanette flipped to the last page. "Those are the worst places," Arthur explained.

"Central Corn Husk Hospital, Chip City, Kansas," Jeanette read. "That sounds like a cozy place, darling."

"It's the worst hospital that hasn't been shut down. But it will be soon. Cornhusk is still under appeal. They have a fourteen percent occupancy rate, and their mortality rate is three standard deviations above the national average."

She agreed that this sounded like quite a deviation.

"Look at their motto." Arthur allowed a small smile. "DOING THE BEST WE CAN WITH WHAT WE'VE GOT."

"How sweet." Jeanette still thought that it sounded like a pleasant place, and the people are probably real homey.

Her husband indicated that those factors did not fit into the formulas, either.

"If you have the operation at Mid Atlantic, Artie, my cousin Grace can keep an eye on you. She works in the dietary department." Jeanette wiggled her fingers through his hair.

Arthur smiled and slicked his hair back in place. "I'm going to have the operation at Roosevelt Memorial Hospital in Danville, Colorado, and the surgeon is Dr. Ernst Lester Colby. He is fifty-three years old, six-foot-one, and one hundred ninety pounds. He doesn't smoke, and he drinks socially. In 1997 he invented the Colby clamp. He has less than a one-percent incidence of post-operative sepsis and had the lowest transfusion rate per surgical hour last year based on patient surface area and pre-operative blood pressure."

"Danville, Colorado," Jeanette repeated. "That's far away. It might cost a thousand dollars to fly there."

"Darling, we are not going to fly. Haven't you been reading the Times? Intelligent people don't fly anymore. We are going to drive. I will get the route lined up tomorrow."

Two weeks later, with the motel reservations placed, hospital admission guaranteed, and the surgeon lined up, the Blankenships packed in preparation for the trip to Colorado. Jeanette thought that if Christopher Columbus had made similar arrangements for his trip west, he would have docked in India on schedule and the Constitution would have been delayed a few hundred years.

"Artie, do we need three tires in the back seat?" Jeanette asked.

"The emergency rations and the flares take up too much room, and the tires won't fit into the trunk. I'll squeeze them between the case of motor oil and the anti-freeze."

After the tire pressure was reconfirmed, they eased off Kennedy Drive and onto the Bushmiller expressway. Arthur didn't have to remind Jeanette that Governor Bushmiller had died at Garfield University Hospital after bowel surgery.

"Wasn't he ninety-four?" Jeanette asked.

"A minor consideration," Arthur responded.

As they proceeded along the highway, Arthur seemed to relax; but periodic grimacing and jaw tightening suggested that the hernia was giving him more difficulty. Jeanette's offer to do some driving was declined.

After two days on the road, or was it three, Jeanette seemed to lose track of her surroundings and dozed periodically. Suddenly, as she drifted into or out of somnolence, she heard a loud scream and saw Arthur grab his groin. As Jeanette straightened up in her seat, the car struck a barrier and turned toward the oncoming traffic.

Fortunately, the car twisted onto the shoulder, away from the flowing traffic. The front of the car was crushed and the hood pointed toward the dashboard. Arthur, with a backseat tire around his neck, was motionless and did not respond to Jeanette's screams. He was wedged between the seat, the tire, the steering wheel and the door; and she couldn't move him. Jeanette, though in the death seat, was uninjured. She felt frightened but no other sensation.

After what seemed like hours but was fourteen minutes, sirens from a State Highway patrol car and an ambulance approached. In a skillful, practiced manner the crew freed the unresponsive actuarial and evaluated him on a stretcher under a light beaming from the van.

"He's starting to stir," one of the medics told Jeanette. "Probably just a concussion, but I think he has a broken wrist; and we better strap him down so he don't hurt himself. Are you okay, Ma'am?"

"Just a little shaken up, but I'm not hurt," Jeanette indicated.

She was told to hop into the ambulance. "We got your husband locked in, and I reckon we better be headin' to the hospital."

Jeanette, tears streaking down her cheeks, stroked Arthur's face gently. He seemed to be resting comfortably. It was all happening faster than she was able to follow. As she held his hand, she wished that her husband were there to tell her what to do. Before she realized it, she was given a seat in the emergency room and a cup of coffee. A nurse told her that Mr. Blankenstrap .....uh.....

Blankerside was on a stretcher in a cubicle and his vital signs were stable. Everything was under control.

The nurse handed Jeanette a form to sign so that the hospital could start treatment. As she shook trying to keep the pen near the 'x', a yawning doctor, or orderly, came from the back, pulled up his sagging pants and explained that Arthur was going to need surgery right away. He had a few broken bones, a collapsed lung and a strangulated hernia that could not wait. "We have three or four pretty good surgeons on the hospital staff. Which one do ya want?" he asked. "They all seem to do kinda decent work."

Jeanette indicated that she was an interior decorator and didn't know anything about picking surgeons. The hospital should choose which one was best for Arthur.

The young man understood; and he would call Dr. Otis Whooten, who had just delivered a calf and probably was still awake and not far out of town.

Jeanette was led into Arthur's room. He was strapped down, but awake with a thin red tube down his nose. His eyes seemed to want to say something, but his mouth couldn't form the words.

Jeanette stroked his forehead and told him not to try to talk. She had taken care of everything, and Arthur was in good hands; there was nothing to worry about. As she spoke, his eyes widened. The sweet, smiling nurse, in a Landfill High School sweatshirt, asked Jeanette to sign some forms. They were permission for treatment in the emergency room, for blood transfusions, for the surgery and for just about anything else that might arise.

"You never can tell what the doctor will find once they get inside." Arthur struggled to get up, but the sweet nurse pushed his chest down with the heel of her hand.

Jeannette, eyes still misty, was shown where to sign. "Everything will be just fine, my dear," the nurse said as she handed Jeanette a tissue. She could not read the name of the hospital or any of the words on the consent forms.

As she smiled and handed the paper back to the nurse, Jeanette, her eyes now dry, did notice the sentence on the bottom of the sheet: "DOING THE BEST WE CAN WITH WHAT WE'VE GOT."

Ron Picker was at the water cooler when Arthur walked by.

"I haven't seen you for quite a while, Artie. You look great," Picker shouted. "You've even got a little pot belly. Did you double up on your megavitamins and bile acid pills?"

"No." Arthur explained that he was no longer taking supplements. "Stopping them helped, but I also had my hernia repaired and a few other medical problems taken care of. I'm eating better and feel great."

"You must miss that old hernia. Where did you get it done?" Picker asked. "At the University?"

"No. A nice little place in Kansas. The people were great, and the food was fabulous." Arthur smiled. "If you ever need surgery, let me know, and I'll tell you about it."

Picker's hemorrhoids were bleeding, but he didn't think he would ever have surgery. "Too many complications."

"Perhaps, but I didn't have any," Arthur boasted as he walked by and stepped into the elevator. "I'm glad I chose it."

THE LAST HOT DOG

"Yes, Mr. Hoddenhold, the statement is quite correct. The total charge for your last hospitalization is only $78,335. We hope that your stay with us was pleasant." John VanCamp talked quickly as he looked directly through the stooped- shouldered client into the waiting room. As always it was full.

"But I was in the hospital for only three days."

"The breakdown of charges is there." VanCamp tapped an enameled finger onto the right hand column. "But don't worry, Sir. Charges have nothing to do with actual cost, and cost has nothing to do with payment. It's very complicated, but you don't pay. The government or your carrier will pick up the bill. The only remaining charge is $114.75 for a strawberry surprise sundae, which was disallowed."

Lester Hoddenhold shook his head and looked like he had just finished another strawberry surprise. "The food was delicious, simply delicious."

"NUMBER 24, PLEASE," VanCamp called out as Hoddenhold waddled off to the right.

A gray-haired woman in a flowery green dress walked slowly into VanCamp's office, leaned over the desk and dropped a white tag with a red number into a half empty coffee cup. Sitting in a chair of modest dimensions, she wedged her shopping bag and cane between her swollen, twisted legs.

"My name is Minnie Weisenfeld, mister. Minnie Gross Weisenfeld." She pulled a wad of papers from her bulging SuperGarfield bag and draped it over a picture of Jennifer, Billy and Buster, the VanCamp children and beagle. "I am here to go over the bill you sent me."

"I know, Mrs. Weisenfeld, so is everyone else in the waiting room." He whirled in his chair. With a few taps on the keyboard, a seven-page printout slivered out of the computer.

"M. G. Weisenfeld, SS 044-43-6748, your total is $67,245. But don't worry you don't…….."

"That's a lot of money for a polyp. I was only in the hospital overnight."

"Well, Madame, hospital costs are going up," VanCamp said as his right hand moved to his calculator. "Let's see, $1450 for peer review and quality assessment, $960 for lunch, $245 for computer paper and ….."

"All I had was a chicken salad sandwich with cranberries. No mayonnaise. It was good, but if I come back, I'll bring my own sandwich."

VanCamp wanted to tell her that she could have her polyp back if she was displeased. "And two hours of operating room time and a $1400 cleanup charge. With today's labor costs, it adds up."

"If you let me clean your operating rooms, sonny boy, it wouldn't add up so fast."

"You don't understand, Ms. Weisenfeld." VanCamp looked at his gold watch. The staff meeting would start in twelve minutes.

"Our Vice-President for Operations and Budget just makes these numbers up. For seniors, either the government or a supplemental pays us based on the disease."

"I didn't have a disease, mister, I had a polyp."

"It doesn't matter. Everyone who is admitted gets a disease assigned." VanCamp spoke quickly. "Then we get paid based on the disease we give you. It doesn't matter how long a client stays or how much it really costs to take care of him. We get the same payment for everyone with the same disease."

"So it's better for you if I croak as soon as I get admitted."

VanCamp agreed. Of course she was right. The customer always is. Although he understood her concerns, he had an important meeting. If she had any more questions, she could come back and take another number.

When VanCamp walked into the paneled boardroom, the corporate officers meeting was in progress; and Larry Williamson was giving an update on the seemingly endless hospital acquisition negotiations.

Their facility, Suburban Community General Hospital, a private investor-owned corporation with 230 beds and a profit of 347 million dollars in 2011, was being purchased by the Jolly Solly Hot Dog Company, a nation-wide chain of fast food restaurants.

"Jolly Solly likes the hospital's financial structure," Williamson told the officers, "but the purchase price will depend on the findings and conclusions of that damned annual Government Mortality Report."

"Although we have the best veal picante and sautéed scallops in the Garfield City area, we also have the highest mortality rate in the regional health district: 0.54 deaths per one hundred patient days. The impact of mortality on our ability to attract private insurance carriers and the value of our stock is obvious." Williams distributed seven graphs and three reports to document the obvious.

The President, Chief Financial Officer and Chief Executive Officer, Garth Neidlander, pushed back in his chair, relit his cigar and thanked Williamson for his report. Other reports followed.

The cost saving committee was finalizing PSTS, the patient self-transport system, that would be operational in July. The Radiology Department was still investigating the feasibility of a debit-card operated X-ray machine in the Harvey Cushing lobby. The dietitian reported that after the take-over, the employee cafeteria would serve only frankfurters, Solly Burgers and Jolly Giant root beer.

Finally, the marketing department chair indicated that they were negotiating with seven more pre-paid health plans, but the final decision would await the Federal Government Mortality Report.

President Neidlander moaned, "Does everything hinge on that report? Why are death rates so important in this business?"

A week later the moment came. President Neidlander lit his cigar and coughed. Everyone at the long mahogany table straightened up.

"Jane is handing out copies of the Federal Government Mortality Report. The conclusions are on page eleven, and the report is quite favorable. Fellow investors, our success is guaranteed."

Everyone turned quickly to page eleven.

"The High Mortality Rate at Suburban Community General Hospital is attributable to overall physician incompetence, inferior equipment, poorly trained personnel and incredible mismanagement."

Everyone smiled, and there was vigorous backslapping around the table. VanClamp and Williamson raised their arms in a victory gesture.

Vindication at last. The hospital was cleared of charges that it was intentionally killing patients to decrease length of stay and increase profits.

"The deaths were simply due to poor patient care," Neidlander indicated. "No one appreciates the importance of shortening hospital stays more than we do, but we did not resort to murder to achieve our goal. That would be bad for business and require approval of the advisory committee. We can meet our goals with absolute incompetence, and we trust that Jolly Solly will not want to change that."

As the officers continued their self-congratulatory chatter, Jane waved a telephone receiver in President Neidlander's face. "Not now Jane. Can't it wait until after the meeting?" No! It was Solomon Siminski, and he cannot wait.

"Who the hell is Solomon Siminski?", Neidlander asked.

When he was reminded that Siminski was Jolly Solly, the room became hushed; and Neidlander listened to the telephone attentively.

Solly had read the report; and, yes, it eliminated concerns he had about criminal conspiracy. It confirmed his belief that the officers of Suburban Community General were not capable of conspiracy. He was ready to meet and close the deal.

On the meeting day, Neidlander and his officers were seated around the thick mahogany table when Jolly Solly walked in. If the crew was disappointed that the short gentleman with the bushy mustache was not wearing his red and yellow piggy suit, it was not obvious.

Neidlander asked Morris Bottomlein, the chief accountant, to review Suburban's view of the health care market.

"Perhaps a contrast with the local University Hospital would be helpful," Bottomlein began. He distributed a report, which indicated that the Garfield City University Hospital had the most sophisticated equipment in the region. And, like Sollyburgers, the best reputation in the state. On the other hand, they had the highest daily costs and the largest annual deficit.

Mr. Siminski understood. While they didn't have the problems facing the University Hospital, wouldn't Suburban's reputation be damaged by the high death rate? While primarily in the food business, he had always thought of hospitals as places intended to help people, to provide medical care.

Bottomlein shook his head. He understood the hot dog king's concern and quaint view of health care delivery. "Clients will not stay away because of the difference between a 0.32 and 0.74 mortality rate," he assured Jolly Solly. "The health plans that buy health care from us are not concerned about those numbers. They sell their programs to businesses primarily on cost."

"And public image is of no concern to you?" Siminski asked.

"Our marketing team can handle that. We'll change the wallpaper, redecorate the lobby and advertise our lobster bisque on television. Have you ever tried it?"

No. Mr. Siminski hadn't tried the bisque. He liked sausage and hated seafood. "What about the doctors? Aren't they concerned about the quality of care of their patients?"

Frankly, Bottomlein hadn't thought about that. It wasn't his area; but since most of the physicians were full-time employees, he doubted that this was a problem. "We're not dependent on private practitioners," Bottomlein explained. "They order too many studies and expensive medications. That's the problem at the university; too many doctors."

Siminski understood. But somewhere in the back of his mind he sensed a flaw in their view of the industry. Yes, he made a fortune by marketing hot dogs wisely; but he thought that he would not have done well if his product wasn't good.

"I've looked over your books," Jolly Solly noted, "and I agree that you are adaptable and have great potential for continued profits."

Everyone smiled. The lawyers huddled as only lawyers can. Eventually the papers were ready, and when the signing was completed everyone applauded as the new owner rose to speak.

"The hospital has been sold at a fair price," he began. "The physical plant is attractive, the parking facilities are adequate and the surrounding area is quite pleasant. Although I do not share your philosophy of management, I'm just an old hot dog vendor; and I have, as you say, a quaint notion that if you don't give value for the dollar, eventually you will go out of business. Since I don't want this to happen to Suburban, I will accept no more patients. When the last patient is discharged and the main building is vacant, we will covert the facility into a luxury hotel and restaurant. The chef is outstanding, and she will be retained."

Solly paused and looked around the room. Every vice-president was silent and motionless. A large gray ash fell from Niedlander's cigar and landed on his lap.

"If any of you are interested in a position at Chez Siminski or at Jolly Solly Hot Dog House, my staff will be happy to consider your application. Does anyone have a question?"

No one did.

THE GREAT SAVE

It was Tuesday, November 17th. The fact that it had rained all afternoon was irrelevant. It was the day that Harry Karmowitz chose to vomit on Mark Littman's white coat and die; the day that Grace Pulanski kicked Littman in the groin as he maliciously drained her bodily essence with an E.K.G. machine. Neither event was unusual.

When it finally stopped raining, the blue and white Blissful Memories Nursing Home van pulled up to the E.R. entrance and unloaded Sam Klinger of Pavilion B with eight of his closest friends. And then there was Johnny Boland, who would not wheeze a minute longer without professional help.

Even the case of Warren the drug addict, who left the better part of his nose in his handkerchief when he blew it, was not especially noteworthy. Although he displayed it proudly on a bloody tissue, he hoped he could grow a new one. He did not want that ugly piece sewn back on.

At the end of the shift, Mark Littman, in need of a shave and shower, flipped on the TV and passed out on the upper bunk while struggling to pry off an infected, blood stained sneaker. He had forgotten to call Katie, his fiancée. Until now it had been a routine day at Maxwell Memorial, aka 'the meat market', but soon to be one that young Dr. Littman would remember forever.

The "meat market", a cluster of grimy brick buildings at Eighth and Baywood, was a Garfield City landmark. Littman had been there for 18 months; the market had been there since the beginning of time, or earlier. It was where Randall Hughes, in a seven-button suit and derby, removed an inflamed appendix, Pennsylvania's first. It was where Winslow Slater Nelson prescribed arsenicals for the treatment of the favorite disease of the gilded age, syphilis; where J.J. Morrison miraculously saved the life of a skinny nine-year-old diabetic girl with an injection of a new purified compound, insulin. That little girl went on to become the cranky old hospital librarian.

It is unlikely that Mark Littman, a graduate of the Irving T. Mehlman Medical College, St. Bruce Island, would have been accepted for a residency in Maxwell's golden age. Nor would any other current medical resident.

Garfield University Hospital and Mid-Atlantic Medical Center, the gleaming downtown institutions, used full-page newspaper ads to highlight the services they will gladly provide to all insured sufferers. Maxwell has never advertised. Most patients arrived in a meat wagon, and insurance was something that storeowners paid to keep their windows and kneecaps from shattering.

Despite the hospital's decline, when Dave Fisher conducted morning rounds on the general medical service, the residents had better know their patients and be up to date on all the right diseases. A few months earlier, for example, Mark Littman had stayed up all night taking care of a guy named Clemmons Buchbrenner. Littman reviewed the case with the chief resident, the nephrology fellow, the file clerk and the gastroenterologist on call. At nine the next morning, he was ready. He hoped.

"Mr. C.B. is a forty-seven year old white, male beer truck driver who was admitted last night with a chief complaint of weakness," Littman remembered saying.

"Weakness? The chief complaint must be a direct quote." Dr. Fisher wondered if those were C.B's exact words.

"Not exactly, sir. He said, 'I feel like shit'," Littman replied. "The patient was a forty-seven year old beer truck driver who felt like shit."

"Better, Mark, but does anyone find anything else wrong with the chief complaint?" the chairman asked his huddled, sleep deprived masses.

"Well.....I would not give his occupation in the chief complaint," smiling Larvid Tushmantal, the chief resident, volunteered.

"In this case, however," Littman responded quickly, "the occupation is relevant. The guy who dropped him off said that his pal Clem, ..uh, ..C.B. sometimes emptied half his truck before his first delivery." Littman smiled. "May I proceed?"

Fisher nodded and Littman continued. "Four minutes after he hit the E.R., he had a generalized seizure and became totally unresponsive. I couldn't get any additional history. I was very upset." The chief understood.

"On examination his respirations were shallow, and he did not withdraw from noxious stimuli, including Tushmantal's socks."

"That is unnecessary," Dr. Fisher reprimanded. "Continue without editorial comment."

"Yes, sir. On physical examination he appeared dehydrated with a blood pressure of 76/50. His liver descended down to his pubis and...."

Fisher turned away from Littman and led the residents, followed by two orderlies and the newspaper boy, into the patient's cubicle, where he attempted to confirm those findings on the lifeless form in front of him.

"What did the initial lab studies show?" the chief asked, as he studied a tattoo of a red fairy princess riding a unicorn on Buchbrenner's freckled right forearm.

"Sir, we repeated the chemistries three times. The man has no electrolytes, no ions.....uh ...he is totally devoid of minerals."

"No sodium, no potassium, no calcium? Impossible. That is unheard of." Fisher dropped his arms and tilted his head toward Littman. "That means that he would have no electrical activity. That is incompatible with life on this planet."

Littman's forehead, which did have electrical activity, beaded with sweat. "Well, I guess that he did have some electrolytes, but the magnesium and phosphorus levels were unmeasurable; and his calcium was so low, that it set a record for the Bircher autoanalyzer."

Dr. Fisher curled his lips in and squinted.

Littman, his eyes bursting with facts, continued with a lengthy explanation of how C.B. developed that degree of chemical depletion. "All his meals came out of a bottle which was low in everything your mother said you needed to grow up big and strong like her. He had no phosphorus or magnesium intake."

"The Lord must have loved phosphorus, he made so much of it," Robert Nachman, self-appointed spiritual leader of the residents, contributed, while swaying.

Dr. Fisher, who appeared to be studying Tushmantel's socks, thought that this was a good note on which to end rounds, and he was down the hall and out of sight before you could say "fluid and electrolyte imbalance."

Littman dashed to the nurses' station, picked up a chart and headed back to Room 207 determined to save limp, crimson Clem Buchbrenner. C.B. reminded him of the hopeless wrecks that Liam Alimazuma, last year's chief resident, brought back from the dead. He never gave up.

As he pushed the door open, Littman wondered what happened to some of Alimazuma's "saves". Littman never saw them in clinic after they left the hospital. Wouldn't it be great if some of them, even just one or two, went on to productive lives? If a patient became a drug counselor or went back to school and became an archbishop or chief justice of the Supreme Court? Or even if some old-timer could live long enough to go to his granddaughter's wedding?

"You have to take them one at a time," Alimazuma always told him. "Don't make judgments. Give every patient your best shot, and what happens, happens." Littman understood. "You cannot play God. Do the best you can."

Now at the bedside, Littman, waking from his daydream, untangled four sets of intravenous lines that led to a catheter in the vein under Buchbrenner's collarbone. Littman had spent the night studying fluid and mineral replacement, and his patient was receiving salt with more precision than the annual federal budget submitted to congress. He turned to the ventilator and adjusted the settings. A few quick pokes left no doubt that his patient was still comatose. Alimazuma was gone, but this worn out battery was Littman's disaster, and he would try to pull him through.

"Look, Katie, I can't make it tonight," Littman whispered into the phone.

"Hey," she shouted, "you must be kidding. We've been planning this for three months, and you are not backing out now!"

"I know, I know, but I've got another really tough case, and I can't leave until I get things straightened out."

"I bought a new dress for this."

"The patient really needs me."

In response to Katie's subsequent high-pitched questions, Mark was explaining that, no, he did not think that he was Jesus Christ, when he heard a sharp click and a hum in his ear. He put the receiver back in the cradle and returned to the article, "Management of Respiratory Failure in Desperately Ill Derelicts" in <u>The Journal of Urban Disasters.</u>

"Turn out the damn light," Chung V. Chung shouted from the lower bunk. "It's three o'clock, you asshole."

Littman admired Chung's mastery of the American idiom.

"Give me a break," Littman responded, a touch of desperation in his voice. "I'm trying to find the best way to manage liver failure. It took two and a half weeks, but we got Buchbrenner off the ventilator. He was starting to wake up when he began flapping like a damn flag. He's yellower than a canary, and his enzymes are off the wall. It's the worst case of liver failure that I've ever seen."

"Turn out the fuckin' light," Chung responded.

"I've already rejected the idea of a liver transplant or exchange transfusions; the guy is too old. Chung, what do you think of the idea of pig liver perfusion?"

"Look, Littman, in my country pig liver is a delicacy. Did you ever try it with bean curd? It's awesome. I'd be dipped in dog turds before I'd waste a perfectly good pig liver on that tattooed slime bucket of yours."

Littman turned out the light and contemplated cross-circulation between Chung and Buchbrenner.

Three weeks later, Marion McDonald, the new second floor nurse, grabbed Mark by the sleeve; and, dragging him to the nurses' station, complained that his sleazy patient in 207 pinched her right breast while she was "cleaning his, er, ...cleaning him."

"He pinched you?", Littman shouted. "He's awake, he's responsive!" Littman dashed down the corridor and into Room 207.

"He's awake.....you're awake," he repeated as he flung the door open. "I'm Doctor Littman; I'm your doctor. I've been working on you for six weeks. Most of the guys said that you were going to die, but I never gave up. Now it looks like you can make it, Clem."

"Wouldya hand me that jar, buddy? I gotta take a leak," Clemmons T. Buchbrenner responded hoarsely, his appreciation somewhat muted, perhaps due to his low potassium level.

Littman reached for the urinal, but then told Clem that he didn't really have to urinate. It felt like it, but he had a tube draining his bladder.

Buchbrenner demanded that Littman pull that damn thing out, along with the crap in his arm, nose and neck.

"Sure. They'll be coming out soon, and we'll get you out of bed."

Littman bounced out of the room thinking about the orders he'd write to get Clem rehabilitated. "Hey, Chung, the guy with the phosphate depletion and liver failure is awake and alert," Littman shouted to his roommate and to an elevator operator when he spotted them at the end of the long corridor. "His B.P. is 120/80, and his 3 P.M. electrolytes were almost normal," Littman announced as he bounced down the hallway. "The guy's gonna make it."

"Hot damn. What a great save," Chung responded, slapping Littman on the back. Arnold, the elevator operator, agreed.

Over the next three weeks Littman watched as his greatest challenge walked the halls, increasing in weight and strength. All his chemistries returned to normal. Finally, Buchbrenner was discharged with prescriptions for vitamins and magnesium, a warning about the evils of alcohol, and an appointment for medical clinic. "And don't forget to eat; phosphorus doesn't grow on trees." Or does it? Littman would look that up.

On the day of Buchbrenner's clinic appointment, Littman was disappointed, but not surprised that he did not show up. They hardly ever do. Maybe Clem was dead. But Mrs. Gebhardt was alive. She was in clinic to show off her purple pyles again. Johnny Greene was there for a codeine refill and any samples that they didn't need. And could Dr. Littman lend him two bucks until Wednesday? But Clem wasn't there, and he wasn't there the next week or the week after that.

As the days passed there were lots of patients. Littman saw two cases of Goodpasture's Syndrome and saved a ninety-four year old lady whose serum potassium was nine with an E.K.G. that was almost a straight line. Although he was busy, Littman still wondered what had happened to his great save. There were other livers, other lungs and other electrolytes. Today, after being kicked and vomited on in the E.R., Mark could finally get to his room, lie down, call Katie and watch the remains of a late ballgame. No reading tonight.

But the ballgame was over, and channel nine had a story with two husky guys running to a car after throwing something red through a store window. Then the guys and the car became fuzzy as Mark drifted away.

As he drifted, Mark was trying to squeeze some grapefruit juice into an I.V. bag, but a clump of seeds blocked the tubing, and Katie was pulling him onto a dance floor. He was wearing roller skates and scrubs. Then his mother told him to go to his room and eat his vegetables. And she looked like Chung. Mark was fairly certain that this had to be a dream.

"I don't have a room," Mark muttered, but suddenly his mother evaporated and a sharp voice startled him. It wasn't Chung or the phone, and it did not seem like a dream anymore. He was no longer wearing roller skates. He was in a dirty shirt and pants and was clutching a sneaker.

"We interrupt this broadcast for a news bulletin. At 6:30 this evening, a truck belonging to the Liberty Brewing Company went out of control on I-59, jumped the median strip and struck a Garfield City school bus traveling north." Mark dropped his sneaker.

"The bus, with students from Clinton Street Elementary, was returning from an excursion to Lansberry Farms." Mark bolted up and rubbed his eyes.

"Police and rescue vehicles are on the scene, and early indications are that nineteen children, a teacher and the bus driver have been injured. The victims have been taken to area hospitals, and the extent of injuries is not yet known."

"The driver of the truck and his passenger escaped with minor injuries and are being held for questioning. The driver, we understand, did not have a valid license and appeared to be intoxicated." Tears rolled down Mark's cheeks. "Clem, no," he cried. "Oh, Clem, no."

"A blood alcohol test was taken, but the results are still pending. We now return to our regular broadcasting. We will break in with additional information as it becomes available."

"It can't be," Mark whispered, looking at the screen.

"......better make a run for it, Stanley. This place is about to blow." Then it blew. Pieces of the building shot across the TV screen

Littman had seen that movie before, and he was dog-tired but wide-awake; his belly was rumbling. At six when the phone rang, he was still awake.

"Morning, Mark. Can you get down here for a minute?" an E.R. nurse asked. "There's a patient of yours here. Bookburner or something like that."

Buchbrenner? He's here? "But what about the accident? What about the police and custody?" he asked.

"Huh? What the hell are you talking about? There are no police. The guy says he just needs a refill of his vitamins and magnesium lactate. What accident? He looks fine to me."

"Nothing," Littman answered, almost laughing. "Nothing. I'll be right down." He raced out of the room holding his sneakers, singing.

"Clem, Clem," he shouted. "It wasn't you!"

A great save doesn't have to become a Supreme Court justice. Staying sober, not ramming your truck into a school bus and taking your meds sometimes can be enough.

ANYTHING YOU CARE TO GIVE

Professor Andrews stood in front of his Economics 204 class. "What would life be like if the economy got so bad that selling body parts was legalized?" he asked. (*)

Donor #1

The policeman, leaning forward with an open pad, asked Johnny to tell him everything.

Johnny had just studied for a geography test and knew all the states surrounding Colorado, the elevation of the Rockies and the population of Flagstaff, Arizona.

"Utah, New Mexi….."

"No, no, son." Sgt. Schwartz closed his pad. "Forget the geography. Tell me what happened after you got home from school?"

"When I got off the bus, I didn't know why Thunderbolt wasn't there." The boy inhaled in stages without breathing out and turned purple. Grace Winslow, sitting next to her son, drew his head against her shoulder. That seemed to reactivate Johnny's breathing mechanism.

"He always waits for me on the corner, and I give him the icky parts of my lunch." Suddenly Grace knew why old "Thunder" was the fattest Golden Retriever in Grand Junction. "And he wasn't in the house, either."

Officer Gilmartin, sitting in a green chair that clashed with his red nose and ill-fitting blue uniform, had his pad wide opened; but his head bobbed rhythmically. His eyes were closed, and he did not react when his pencil fell and rolled under the chair. Earlier, when they were driving to the house, he mentioned to the sergeant that this complaint would be better handled by the S.P.C.A.; but Sgt. Schwartz reminded him that the society did not have a detective division.

"So I went outside to look for him," Johnny continued.

The boy, with blond hair, freckles and drooping ears, looked a bit like a golden retriever. As he spoke, his eyes drooped as well.

"And you found him in the driveway?" Sgt. Schwartz anticipated.

Mom answered for Johnny, who threw his arms around her and shrieked loud enough for Gilmartin to open his eyes and look for his pencil. Barney the cat had already walked off with it. "We found him right outside the garage door."

"Did he say anything?" Gilmartin asked.

"No! Thunderbolt was dead," she said. "He's still where Johnny found him."

"Let's go out and have a look," Sgt. Schwartz suggested.

Even a casual observer of the corpse would have been satisfied that this was not an accidental death. Nor was it, despite Officer Gilmartin's theory, a suicide. The large, limp dog was lying in a pool of congealed blood with his tongue pasted against the pavement. Gilmartin wondered if Thunderbolt, like his late Aunt Louise, had a coagulation defect. The source of the blood loss, however, was obvious. The dog's neck had been sliced from under the angle of the right jaw to the left ear.

"Did Thunderbolt have any enemies?" Gilmartin asked. Mrs. Winslow thought that there was a Doberman on Ninth and Chichester that didn't seem to care much for him. She did not know why. Thunderbolt had some bad habits, but for the most part he was an introspective and considerate fellow. All the animals on the block respected him, almost as much as Johnny did.

Sgt. Schwartz knew the type. And he doubted that most Dobermans carried the sort of knife needed to create that large gash.

"Just what kind of animal would do this, Sarge?" Officer Gilmartin asked.

The sergeant pulled Gilmartin's right ear toward his mouth and whispered something about focusing on possible human suspects. Gilmartin shook his head slowly; and, for the first time, a knowing look crossed his face.

"Dognapping and burglary are common in the area, but why," Schwartz asked, "would someone slash a poor beast and let him bleed to death in his own driveway?" The assailant or assailants had made no attempt to break into the house or deface the property.

"Thunderbolt was hardly a watch dog," Mrs. Winslow added.

The sergeant spotted a small wound on the animal's belly and pushed his right foot under the dog's trunk and flipped him over.

Sgt. Schwartz was glad that Johnny was inside the house. The small wound on the belly was just the edge of an arching incision that split open the dog's right flank and most of his abdomen. This gash, like the one in the neck, was filled with a gelatinous clot. The edges of the wound were sealed by that clot, and only later, in the pound, was the full depth of the incision appreciated;

and only then was it noted that a number of internal organs were missing.

Donor #2

Johnny J. Megalick was not the type of man that one would fail to notice. Through no fault of his own, his head was large and accentuated by his narrow shoulders and long thin neck. But more than its size was his head's glow and excrescences. His shaved head called attention to the ridges, small masses really, that started where a hairline often begins and continued to where it generally ends. His misaligned nose was large, too, but not quite as shiny.

Then there were the earrings and flashy clothes. He liked red shirts, gold necklaces, white ties and pointy-toed shoes with three-inch heels.

"I got da five 'G's, Augie," Megalick announced, as he pulled an envelope out of his back pocket and dropped it on the desk. "Dat should settle our account."

Despite the heels, since Megalick was little more than four feet tall, the money didn't have far to drop.

"That don't settle shit, you little runt," Augie Moore corrected as he spit something dark and wet out of the corner of his mouth. "I don't know where you got this dough, but you still owe me ten big ones."

Augie, leaning over his desk, hardly looked more imposing than Megalick, but the guys standing behind him did. These two gentlemen seemed totally focused on looking angry. Megalick assured all three that he had a good deal going and would make full payment, including interest, shortly. "Make that very shortly. It's a sure thing."

"I heard that one before." Augie, leaning forward a bit more, grabbed Megalick's red collar and pulled him over the edge of the desk so that their noses were touching. "The only sure thing is gonna be you in a garbage bag in the city dump. Why don't you quit gambling while yer still breathing?"

"Hey, I didn't get the money gambling. What I'm doing now ain't gambling – it's a sure thing, professional, and I'm good for the cash. Just give me a little time."

Augie let go of the shirt, and his client dropped to his feet. Megalick's collar was torn; and his tie, stained with ashes, was pulled out of his vest and looped over his shoulder. Augie squinted, drawing his face around his bulbous nose, and crushed the cigar in an ashtray. The guys behind him did not move or blink.

"I got another five grand coming by the end of the month." Megalick held his hands in front of his chest to dissuade "the Aug" from grabbing his clothes again. "Guaranteed."

"Where ya getting it?" Augie wondered.

"Business."

"What kinda business ya in? Dwarf tossing?"

"It's medical stuff. I'm in the kidney business." He smiled. His mother would be proud, but Augie's expression did not improve.

"Look, Aug, there's a big market for small kidneys, and I'm what ya call a pea-de-atric donah."

"Pediatric, my ass. Last year it was the car business, and ya fenced ya brudder-in-law's car when he was outta town."

"This is different. This is my own stuff. I get two grand for every kidney I donate."

"And how many have you donated?"

"So far, just four or five."

Surgeon #1

J.J. Gladstone was sitting at the bar; it was almost three o'clock. He held out as long as he could, and Bella knew where to find him if she needed him. Although the place was almost empty, J.J. spotted a potential companion and sat down next to her. The young lady, turning her head away, acted as though she was visually impaired.

"Do you come here often?" he asked. He usually had a better opening, but he was tired, rushed and distracted.

The young lady, without looking at him or responding, stood and walked out. No doubt she had detected that hidden something special in Gladstone. Perhaps the cologne, the sunglasses in the dark room or the perfect streak of gray in his charcoal hair.

"It's the damn job," he muttered. It was better than the last one and tailored to his qualifications. It required a medical background, which he had, but did not require a medical license, which he no longer had. He'd had several state licenses over the years, but none recently, and little chance of ever getting another.

Al, the bartender, came over to Gladstone. Although he mixed a lousy martini, Al knew the principals of surgery and had a list of questions for J.J. about pre-op antibiotics, CT scans and the tensile strength of synthetic suture material.

"Al, you know that I have not been near an operating room in twelve years," J.J. pleaded.

Al did know. He knew that J.J. had been accused of operating under the influence of something, simply because he passed out twice during preliminary sponge counts. That never stopped Al from asking. He didn't get many transplant surgeons in the bar.

Unfortunately, J.J.'s cell phone rang during the first question. Bella wanted to know where the hell he was and told him to contact his office. He had two messages.

"Some guy from your medical school called and wanted to know if you could make the class reunion. The twenty-fifth."

J.J. was sorry he missed the call. The last time someone called from the medical school, he was still in Nelson Whytecollar Correctional. Might have been from prescribing controlled substances in bulk without examining the patients. He wanted to show his old classmates that he was back in circulation.

"The guy's name was Fisher," Bella continued. "He thought he was calling Oregon, because, when I picked up the phone, I said 'Thanks for Calling the Organ Bank'. This is Junction City, Colorado, I said. Haven't you heard of the JG Organ Bank, supplier of vital parts to America's sick and ailing?"

" 'Sure I heard of you,' " he tells me. " 'Aren't you the first commercial supplier of hearts, kidneys and livers?' He knew that we went into business as soon as the sale of body parts was legalized."

J.J. wondered if Bella could get on with it.

"I told him we also had eyes, lungs and pancreases available and would be happy to send him a brochure," Bella continued to explain. "But, 'no, thanks' he says, he's in medical education. A neurologist. If we sold brains, he'd be interested. But he was just calling about the reunion and just wanted to talk to his classmate."

"Okay, and the other call?" J.J. pleaded.

"That was from Jack Skinner. Said that you would know where to reach him."

"Skinner," he repeated. Gladstone thought that he better get back to the office. He wanted to speak to Fisher, but knew that he had to call Skinner.

The Recipient

Ronnie never wanted to open the door when the bell rang. Always, or almost always, the man or woman at the door would choke on their tongue, say "Hello" as if it were a new word with too many consonants and then pull back and squint at Ronnie the way you'd look at someone with an extra nose.

"Are you….uh…you must be Ronnie?"

Some at the door knew that he was thirteen, and some knew that he was in the eighth grade. But being shorter than his nine year old sister surprised them. Or maybe they were reacting to his bowed legs and pigeon chest. Maybe it was the big words coming out in a squeaky little voice.

"Hello," the stranger repeated, better with practice. "I'm Jack Skinner. I think that your parents are expecting me."

"So am I," Ronnie replied. "Please come in."

Skinner, once the director of an organ donation center, was the consultant for many charitable funds and should not have been startled by the appearance of a boy who'd had kidney disease since he was four. But lots of things about Ronnie surprised people, even his doctors.

Number one: being first in his class, despite many missed school days and dialysis treatments. Number two: keeping a newspaper route. Three: being a boy scout with eleven merit badges.

Led into the living room, Skinner joined Ron's parents and seven or eight other normal-sized adults without renal rickets, who were chatting, looking at papers and drinking a variety of liquids without recording the volume. Ron, on the other hand, having reached four hundred milliliters by three o'clock, just sucked on a piece of low potassium raspberry hard candy.

"Have a seat, Jack. Nice to see you," Allan Kennedy, Ron's dad said, and sounded as though he meant it.

The adults, including Garfield City's most progressive, guilt-ridden middle class, were meeting for the third time as "The Ronald Kennedy Kidney Fund". They needed direction, a leader and forty thousand dollars before their favorite scout could get a kidney transplant.

Allan Kennedy explained, again, that no one in the family was a suitable match. He did not want to explain why, since he had never told Ronnie that he was adopted. Ronnie, however, who had studied genetics, reached that conclusion when he was nine but did not want to alarm his parents.

Last month Ron explained to his friend, Warren, "Since each parent contributes half of their genes, I couldn't be a total antigen mismatch with either of them if they were my biological parents." Louis wished that he were adopted, too. Then he would not be at risk of growing up like his father. He didn't know anything about antigens, but he already had his father's nose and overbite.

The fund people knew that if either parent were a match, they would certainly give a kidney or a good chunk of it to Ronnie. "Furthermore," Allan added, "we are just too big." That was not meant as a boast. Ronnie, short of sixty pounds, needed a small kidney, from another child or an unrelated little adult.

Next came the money issue. "Why aren't the costs covered by insurance?" someone asked. This was where Jack Skinner's expertise came in. "When it was legalized, and people started selling their organs, the market on free ones dried up. No one is going to give away a body part that they can sell for big bucks. The insurance companies will pick up surgical bills but backed away from the organ market. No plan pays for the purchase of parts. Hearts, kidneys, lungs, eyes: it's all the same."

People were warned that this would happen, but not how far it would go, especially cashing in on the organs of dying relatives. Like the case of Jasper Wilson. Everyone on the committee knew that one. Jasper was written into his Aunt Margaret's will as the recipient of her cottage in East Fruita, the 1802 Royal Vienna Clock, her cat, Amber, and all her bodily remains. Two weeks after the will was notarized, Margaret was in Mid-Atlantic on a respirator after a suicide attempt.

"Left a type-written suicide note and an e-mail," a committee member noted. "Her beloved Cincinnati Horned Toads lost the super bowl, Margaret wrote, and she could not go on any longer."

"Wilson collected over a hundred thousand on her chest contents alone," Skinner added. "Then they booked him for murder."

Talk, talk, talk and sipping drinks continued. Ronnie fell asleep on his mother Adele's lap. When he woke up, all the strangers except Mr. Skinner were gone. Skinner's jacket was off, and he was leaning into Allan Kennedy's face. "Adults are tough enough, but there is too much competition for good little kidneys. They are going to the highest bidder; and if you don't have fifty thousand, the boy will die before he gets one." They must have thought that Ronnie was still asleep. His neck and shoulders hurt, but he didn't move.

"How can we get that kind of cash?" Adele asked, a few tears running down her cheeks. Skinner wanted to stage a phony theft of the fund to create sympathy and build up donations. The Kennedys didn't think that they could go along with that.

"Been done lots of times," Skinner assured them. He did not understand their reluctance. "Okay, I'll keep on working on the supply end. I have the inside track on an achondroplastic dwarf. He is a real humanitarian, and I think I can get his price down."

Skinner would get a blood sample to make sure that there was no mismatch. Adele stopped crying; and Ronnie thought that this was a good time to open his eyes, scratch his shoulder and go to bed.

The fund did not raise fifty thousand dollars for the little kid with the big head despite a dance at Benjamin Harrison High School and several car washes. They had three thousand eight hundred and Ronnie was not doing well on dialysis.

"These amateur car washes are the devil's curse. If one more person in town needs a transplant or a by-pass," Jack Truglight, owner of the Soft as Velvet Car Wash, complained, "I'm out of business."

"Better plan on a transplant within the next four months," Dr. Bowser, the pediatric transplant surgeon, warned. He would do it at the University Children's Hospital. Ronnie did not want to give up the newspaper route, but he had to. Then he didn't have the strength to make it to the Preston Motley Middle School. Finally, he could barely stay awake for his mom's lessons.

The committee, too embarrassed to drink the Kennedy's wine and nibble the cheese and crackers, stopped meeting. But Skinner never lost interest. "Look into a second mortgage on the house," he advised. Since Ronnie had been sick for almost seven years, there was no equity on the house; but Adele had sisters and cousins. Between them and Allan's boss, they got a fifty thousand dollar loan that could be paid back monthly: forever.

"Great. Now," Skinner promised, "we'll get that little kidney for our boy. The donor, a man named Megalick," he told the Kennedys, "is twenty five hundred miles away in Colorado; and they'll ship the kidney in a perfusion box." He thought that they could get it for just forty five thousand (leaving ten percent for his broker fee). "According to the reports, the donor is in great shape. Runs marathons with incredible times for a little person. He's got a doctoral degree in cultural anthropology and writes poetry."

Surgeon #2

The kidney arrived at the airport just as Ronnie was being wheeled into the operating room. "We're with you, doll," one of the nurses shouted as Ronnie rolled past. An orderly gave him a high five, and a few ladies kissed him enroute.

Dr. Kathy Goodwin, a fourth-year surgical resident, had prepped the field, made the initial incision and dissected down to the blood vessels when Bowser, the transplant surgeon, pushed the door open with his hip and walked to the O.R. table with his hands in the "I'm sterile" position. The stereo in the corner, which was playing the Sibelius Symphony No. 2, was turned off; and the circulating nurse dropped in one of Bowser's country hits C.D.s "I loved you till ya left me; then I loved you even more. Why'd you hafta pick up your bowling ball and walk out the door."

"Nice work, Kath," Bowser said as he dropped his hands into a pair of gloves. "The artery looks good. I'll bring the kidney over. How can you listen to that classical crap?", he asked as he placed the kidney on a tray and opened the towel that held it. "Those concertos constipate me." No one wanted to point out that it was a symphony.

"Does the kidney look a little weird to you?" Goodwin asked as Bowser turned it, set it in the child's groin and spread the blood vessels and ureter.

Bowser shrugged his shoulders. "It ain't always gonna look like the ones in your surgical texts. I bet that Beethoven's kidneys looked worse than this one."

"I mean it has a lump at either end, and its shape is a bit strange," she persisted.

"Look, DOCTOR, the thing is pink and firm as a rock. It don't have to win a beauty contest. It just has to piss for the little kid. It wasn't a great match, but the damn thing perfused well, and we're sewing it in and getting out."

Now it was Goodwin's turn to shrug. She asked for vascular scissors and started to trim the edges of the renal artery.

"I don't think that you'd look this pink after flying twenty five hundred miles in freight on Grandview Airlines."

".....I gave you a warm heart, and you gave me a cold shoulder," the C.D. complained as Bowser and Goodwin worked away in the groin. "Why'd you walk out the door?"

"I wonder what Johnnie Cash's kidneys looked like?" the scrub nurse asked. While no one around the table answered directly, Dr. Bowser thought that Sibelius might have written some pretty good western tunes if he'd been brought up right.

Fifty-four minutes later, after Pennsylvania politicians, inflation and reverse mortgages had been discussed and excoriated, a few yellow drops trickled out the trimmed end of the ureter before it was sewn into Ronnie's bladder.

"Well, I hope that stuff is good enough for you, Goodwin," Bowser said. "I'll let you finish up." He left the O.R., and Sibelius returned.

The Little Organ

Kathy Goodwin had taken care of quite a few pediatric recipients, but this one had her puzzled. It wasn't that Ronnie didn't look well. One day after surgery, he looked better than he had in six months. "What I don't understand," Goodwin said to Bowser on the fourth post-op day, "is his urine output. The chemistries are fine, so he must be excreting all his waste products."

"Exactly," Bowser replied, "The kid is in balance."

"But," Goodwin sputtered, "he's doing it with very little output."

"Maybe the nurses aren't recording all of it," Bowser shot back.

Ronnie still had a bladder catheter, and Goodwin knew that the full output was being noted. "And look at this." She waved a computer printout in front of Bowser's face. "The urine osmolarity is twenty-four hundred."

"Twenty-four hundred," Bowser repeated, his face twisted as if he were listening to a Bach Brandenburg Concerto.

"That's right, twice as concentrated as any human kidney can achieve," she said. "Only horses, dogs and desert rats can do that."

"Lab error," Bowser rebutted.

"I checked it myself, four or five times. Twenty four to twenty six hundred every time."

"Look, I'm just a surgeon. I just put 'em in. No one ever complained before that the kidney was working too well."

Two days later, the urine output, scant as best, stopped completely. "The B.U.N. is up to 47," the head nurse reported. "And Ronnie's temperature is 102.4."

Ronnie Kennedy, surrounded by moist-eyed, sniffling nurses, smiled as Dr. Goodwin examined the surgical site.

"We probably have to give up on it," Bowser said on rounds, twelve days after surgery. "But first let's get a biopsy."

The pathologist noted that this was the most extensive rejection reaction she had ever seen. "The tissue is so distorted, it doesn't even look like a human kidney."

By the time the surgeons removed it the following morning, the kidney was blue, twice its original size and popping through its capsule. There was no music or chatter in the O.R. that morning. Whatever the staff thought about the $45,000 that the Kennedys paid for the organ that was cut out of the child's groin and shipped to pathology in a pan was left unsaid.

True Rejection

If Allan and Adele Kennedy had any thoughts about the kidney dying before the first payment was due, they did not mention them. If they had any questions for the surgeons, they did not ask them.

After the excision, Dr. Bowser had another case; and Dr. Goodwin met the Kennedys in the waiting room. Dr. Goodwin and the parents cried together. "Ronnie loves you," Adele said to the surgical resident as she squeezed her hand. "You could not have been closer or done more for him than you did. Please do not blame yourself."

If the Kennedys had any questions for Jack Skinner, they could not ask them. They would never see the "broker" again.

Dr. Goodwin had questions for her chief. Was he going to report this unusual complication?

"What complication are you talking about? It's just a rejection of an unrelated kidney. Happens every day of the week," he shot back.

"Yes. But not after functioning above human capacity."

Bowser closed his eyes and shrugged his shoulders with his palms up.

"And the pathologist thought that it was the strangest looking kidney tissue she had ever seen."

"She's not exactly the world's sharpest renal pathologist, is she?"

"And it looked strange to me in the O.R."

Bowser's eyed popped open. "Look, lady, drop it. It was a tough break, and we all feel bad for Ronnie. But what's done is done. What good does it do to keep batting this thing around?" Bowser's neck veins bulged out from his scrub shirt, and his forehead was covered with sweat. "The kidney was perfect when I put it in. Perfect. Drop it."

He was the chief. She dropped it – for the moment.

Another Fund Raiser

"We appreciate your coming all the way to Cincinnati," Gail Washburn said. Her husband echoed her feelings. Their friend Allison, who knew how desperate they were, told them about Jack Skinner.

"Jennifer is our only child."

"First thing, folks, is that you have got to think positive," Skinner smiled. "We are going to raise the money for her kidney transplant. I guarantee that, one way or another, we are going to come up with the money."

Furthermore, Skinner assured them that he worked closely with brokers at an organ bank, and he had the inside track on a kidney from a social anthropology professor in Colorado. "He is a fabulous little person who needs cash badly. Something about supporting a sick mother."

(*) This story, while anticipating the practice, pre-dated the current, often illegal and sinister, sale of human organs in the International market

BEHIND CLOSED DOORS

An Inside View of the Mysterious World of Academic Medicine

Jack Cameron (aka Jackson Cameron, M.D., M.B.A., M.P.H., Ph.D., F.A.C.P.) ripped the boards from the frame, pounded the padlock with a mallet and tried to ram his right fist through the door. To no avail. It was obvious to a growing crowd that Jackson Althouse Cameron, Senior Editor of the *Journal of Rare Renal Diseases* and the Whelan P. Harrison Professor of Internal Medicine and Chairman of the Department, had been locked out of his office.

Until that moment, no one who watched as Cameron was carried away with a broken right hand and broken left foot would have guessed that his tenure at the Mid-Atlantic College of Medicine would end this way.

Two and a half weeks earlier, this twisted battered remnant, in his fourth academic position, seemed indestructible and bound for glory. Two and a half weeks ago, in this tall building with more committees than windows and more associate professors than janitors, Jack Cameron had four secretaries, five research protocols, a business manager, the third largest office and two windows.

The distribution of books, papers, journals and kitchen utensils in that office suggested that the occupant was immersed in a consuming interest, undistracted by the mundane elements of hygiene and housekeeping. A copy of <u>Garfield City Today</u> with a bony Jackson Cameron looking into an unilluminated microscope over the caption, "Ten Super Stars to Watch in 2009", was spread across a mound of reports and journals anchored in place by a computer keyboard and a dried out sesame bagel.

This professional mess was the subject of ongoing speculation. A few imaginative medical residents, in a lighter moment, speculated that Cameron, to prove his manhood, had strangled one of their colleagues and buried him under the rubble in the far corner. Despite the feasibility of this theory, most senior faculty did not believe that there were concealed human remains on Cameron's carpet. They thought that their chief subscribed to a management technique in which he stayed at a job until his desk was no longer detectable. While his secretary, Marlene Minifield, did not doubt the murder theory, she would not penetrate the office deeply enough to confirm it.

It was quite different when old Doc Bennett had been chairman. Marlene knew where every index card and letter was filed. Now, just nine months after Arnold Bennett's departure, no hint of his sixteen years of benign, paternal, colorless stability remained.

Bennett's desk, the victim of academic politics, was on its side in the basement storage room; and Bennett was on his side on a beach, under a palm tree, 1400 miles south. New diplomas, photographs and awards covered the marks and stains of old diplomas, photographs and awards.

A blue and gold Venezuelan Legion of Merit Award had replaced the picture of Betty and Arnie Bennett with Marvie, the Labrador Retriever, and Billy, the grandson. The 2001 photograph of a smiling, rumpled Arnie Bennett in a blue cardigan, surrounded by twenty-six smiling medical residents, was replaced by a non-smiling Jackson Cameron in a morning coat, looking squarely into the camera while shaking hands with the Norwegian Minister of Health.

Two and a half weeks ago, after nine days in Zurich as a member of the International Renal Disease Commission, Jackson Althouse Cameron, "Outhouse" to the senior class, walked into the tall building, up three flights of stairs and toward his office without acknowledging the wide path that cleared as he advanced. "Jill, get me Burt Phillips, stat," he barked at Marlene as he walked through the outer office. Marlene wondered why his mother never taught him to say "hello" or "good morning" as she leaned reluctantly into his office to remind him that a Herald-Examiner crew was coming at eleven to photograph the story, "New Blood in an Old Institution."

Marlene was sent off to find a white lab coat and a stethoscope for the shoot as he threw a mug off his chair and sat down under two columns of mail. He picked up the right-hand column, local and institutional junk, and threw it in the trash. He spread the out-of-town and international mail, the left-hand column, across his desk and started to read an e-mail from Tokyo when Burt Phillips materialized at his door.

"We have three unfilled residency slots for 2010", Cameron shouted into the message from Japan. Burt said that he knew it and was explaining that he had no explanation when Cameron picked up the phone and asked Jane (aka Marlene) to get Professor Watanabi at the Tokyo Glomerular Disease Institute. Marlene said that she would try as Cameron dropped the receiver and told Burt that he was the residency program director and he damn well better fill those vacancies or he'd be directing enemas in South Schwainsville.

Burt explained that he would have a better chance of getting recruits if the chief was around to interview candidates, since everyone knew Jackson Althouse Cameron, and no one knew Burton Rodney Phillips. Whereupon Cameron flipped two letters and a journal onto the floor and told Marlene to get Danny Wilson with the converting enzyme results. He had to see them immediately. Phillips shuffled his feet, cracked his knuckles and coughed to prove to Cameron and to himself that he was still in the office. "Do you have a cold?" Cameron asked as he walked past Phillips, through the door and into the research lab where Danny Wilson was struggling to pick up an overstuffed notebook from the floor. "You should have had that ready for publication three weeks ago, Davey", he said to Danny.

"Why does the whole place shut down when I'm away?" he asked. Danny tried to explain that he couldn't review Phase II treatment because Dr. Cameron, sir, had taken the protocols and the logbook to Europe. "Look, Donny, I'm not paying you for excuses," the Distinguished Professor rebutted as he turned and walked out of the lab. "You're not paying me at all," Danny muttered to the door that Cameron slammed in his face.

Cameron headed back to the office as Burt Phillips escaped unnoticed. "Get Charlie Castle over here," Cameron demanded as he pushed several letters aside until he came to an invitation to speak at the International Society of Infectious Disease Symposium in Paris. He was dictating his acceptance and a series of recommendations regarding the guest speakers, the program, the banquet location, the lunch menu and the weather when Charlie Castle approached his desk.

Charlie was about to say "hello" when Cameron told him that he would find a new chief resident, if Castle, the ungrateful turd, didn't want the honor and the responsibility. He didn't plan on standing over him every minute to see that he was doing his job, and why weren't those lazy, stupid residents showing up for morning report. Castle wondered how Cameron knew where the residents weren't, but not enough to ask.

Cameron reminded young Charlie Castle that he'd been on call every other night when he was a resident, did his own E.K.G.s, stained his own blood smear and still had time to write the best chapter in Hargraves "Principles of Medicine" and show up on time for morning report. As Castle started to respond, Cameron got up, walked away and asked Marlene why she lost Watanabe. Cameron returned to his office and picked up the next letter, which had a Mid-Atlantic logo and, clearly, was in the wrong stack. He cursed and started to squeeze it to death until he saw that it was from the Chairman of the Board of Directors. His face blanched as he noticed that the phrases had an ominous tone. "The Board of Directors takes pride in your international reputation…..pleased with your position on the editorial board of…your continuing leadership in nephrology research……the Board is re-evaluating its priorities……benefit from a change in emphasis……require modifications to the faculty….express our thanks for your service to Mid-Atlantic….regret we will not be renewing your contract…to avoid conflict….termination effective immediately."

Before the falling letter reached the desk top, Cameron turned crimson, whirled in his chair, hurled his coffee cup, avulsed the phone from its cradle and demanded to talk to that senile, pompous Chairman Waterson as Charlie Castle fell on his face trying to avoid the coffee cup.

Waterson wondered why Cameron hadn't called sooner, and Cameron wondered who the toads on the board thought they were dealing with. He was the best damn thing that ever happened to second-rate Mid-Atlantic. He had too much support on four continents and three islands; heads would roll. Waterson might go, but old Jack wasn't quitting. If they wanted to get rid of him, they damn well better lock him out of his office and be ready to fight. Cameron slammed down the phone, shouted for Jane to get Watanabe as he reviewed his e-mail.

"I'm heading for a meeting in Paris tomorrow," he reminded Marlene, "and I'll deal with Waterson and his bluff when I get back."

THE SINKING SHIP

On a cold and rainy night, two Garfield City Police Officers found Anita Scutter Barksdale unconscious in an abandoned building on East Street and delivered her rigid body and crinkled paper bags to an unconcerned and ungrateful Mid-Atlantic Hospital emergency room staff.

Anita's recuperative powers were well known to the Mid-Atlantic doctors and nurses. When Mark Littman, the medical resident, ventured into the pungent cubicle, the smiling toothless lady with silver-and-orange braids was leaning on her bony elbow and daintily devouring the back end of a dry chicken. The patient's right leg, hanging over the side rail, was immediately recognized as the source of the caustic aroma that infiltrated the room and slithered down the hallway. When Littman pulled the boot from that swollen, ulcerated leg, a rat flew out, slid down the wall and landed on the cold tile floor.

Had the rat been able to talk, he would have expressed regret at having crawled into Anita's black vinyl boot rather than one of her benign paper sacks. But the handsome brown rat, with a finely taped tail, large ears and striking red eyes, was dead.

Typically, since the victim was not human, resuscitation was not considered; and no attempt was made to notify the family. A post-mortem examination, justified only by flimsy public health considerations, was performed without permission of the next of kin and devoid of respect for the dignity of the deceased.

Based on the clinical presentation, crush injuries, including a subdural hematoma, had been considered the most likely cause of death. The autopsy, however, demonstrated that the rat had actually died of asphyxiation long before Barksdale shoved her macerated leg into the deadly footwear. Undoubtedly, the rat's sensitive, irritated lungs had filled with fluid depriving him of oxygen.

The environment in Anita Barksdale's boot was, indeed, quite toxic. The rat, unlike his host, was found to be free of infection. Finally the animal was cremated with assorted debris and tossed into a pit on the grounds of the Patterson Avenue Incinerator and Municipal Dump.

The untimely death of the dapper, young and previously healthy rat, and his burial with an assortment of animal parts and inanimate objects was but one in a series of well-documented animal abuse cases in Garfield City. To address this growing problem, a large group of prominent area rats gathered in a fashionable downtown sewer beneath Kenilworth Avenue.

"These senseless murders and indignities have got to stop," declared Wade Snipper, the aging but none-the-less dignified *rattus norvegicus* behind the podium. "We have pursued a policy of peaceful coexistence with all mammals, and yet we now find ourselves the prime target of Man." His jowls no longer had the handsome puffiness greatly admired during his acting career. "Why, my friends, have we been singled out by these creatures for ridicule and extinction?"

"We won't stand for it!" a tall, red-hooded chap bellowed. And he related a barbarous tale of his dear aunt, Agnes Choppy, who had been poisoned with warfarin in the Municipal Office Center and left to bleed to death while scores of human bystanders callously watched without offering to help. "How many women merely screamed and ran away as the blood poured out of my poor aunt's mouth, I shall never know."

"Why us? and "Why now?" many in the audience cried, their words bouncing off the brick walls and echoing down pipes and drains. Mr. Snipper, sweating under the lights, raised his paw for silence.

"As many of you know, this tailless primate rabble, erroneously referred to as civilization, is once again in great trouble," he explained, removing and wiping his glasses for effect. "Throughout history large primates have looked to scapegoats for their failures. With all due respect to goats, that is what we have become to our human brothers."

"Yes, we are Man's scapegoat," Wade Snipper repeated as he stood below the **"Coalition Against Ratocide"** banner. "We have been blamed for the spread of every disease from anthrax to zoster. Does Man not recognize that we, too, are victims of these diseases?"

"Right on, Rodents, right on!" many enraged rats shouted, thrusting their forelegs in the air.

"Surely, our human colleagues must know that we would rather be with our brothers and sisters in the fields and marshes," the inspired leader continued. There was no need to point out that few fields and marshes remained. "And was it not Man himself who lured us to his land with purulent conditions of urban decay, putrefaction and waste? We must not be blamed for thriving in these succulent places that Man has created."

"This is not the lifestyle of our choosing," Snipper continued, rising on his hind legs and pounding on the podium, bringing to mind his lead role in "Of Mice and Rats". "Are we to be blamed for being adaptive and resourceful?"

"If the biped beasts want to be rid of us, why don't they simply change the way they live?", Dr. Ansel Gray Mist, a professor of human behavior, asked rhetorically. "If they remove our food and rubble, if they seal their deserted buildings, and repair the roofs, we will leave. We would have no choice."

Heads shook and tails fluttered. A large rat in the back raised his paw and was recognized. "And, sir," he asked, "what about the thousands of our brothers and sisters imprisoned in laboratories for frivolous hare-brained (*) notions without regard to their rights or basic comforts? Who among us has not had a friend or neighbor die in the torture chambers of the Mid-Atlantic Medical Center or the Garfield City University without legal representation? Clearly their experiments have not been designed to benefit rodents."

"Perhaps we should use the same public relations techniques that have helped the image of squirrels, chipmunks and gerbils?" Angus Mugsy, the soft-spoken director of Another Rat for Peace asked.

"I'm afraid it's too late for that, Angus. Please don't delude yourself into expecting humans to behave in a compassionate or rational manner. That is without precedent. In fact, they have already led countless innocent species on the road to extinction," Dr. Gray Mist explained. "Furthermore, our problems are just the tip of the iceberg. Incredibly, as the human race prepares for our destruction, they are simultaneously preparing their own."

Suddenly, all rumbling and teeth gnashing in the auditorium stopped; brochures and programs closed, and there was a frightening silence. Every tail was still.

"Yes, my friends, unlike any other mammal, man has engaged in practices and developed instruments for his own complete and total extinction, and, in fact, for the destruction of the entire planet – all at great expense and personal sacrifice. And they push forward," he added, "despite warnings from the few wise souls among them."

Many knew about human behaviors causing global warning, with problems extending well beyond Garfield City and its suburbs including melting glaciers, flooding coastlands, torrential storms and devastating tornadoes. In addition, the decaying infrastructure and its consequences, which will compound the devastation, are barely acknowledged or addressed.

"The growing disparity in health and wealth is also a threat," an Eastern Rodent University anthropology major shouted out. "Yes, but not as much a threat as terrorism and weapons of mass destruction," Mr. Mugsy countered. "There are still many nuclear weapons on this planet that could fall into the wrong hands. As community leaders, you must know that the human efforts at self destruction will threaten all of us."

Heads shook as a sense of doom filled the sewer. Finally, a young Eastern Woodrat asked what could be done about it.

"I see nothing we can do to stop Man's destructive impulses," the somber leader confessed. "We must fall back on our age-old ability to desert sinking ships."

The sewer filled with shouts and screams, almost blowing the cover off the main entrance. "To what ship do you refer?" someone asked. "Do you intend to leave this planet?"

"Yes, precisely. Our success throughout recorded history has been based on our ability to find the most suitable environment.

Today, my dear friends, that means we must go to Mars. And depart before it is too late."

"MARS!" The noise increased as young and old rats dashed about. "MARS!" A few dug their teeth into the walls or scratched rusting pipes. "How are we to get there?"

Wade Snipper's response could not be heard above the noise. He turned away and chose not to think that his friends and associates were behaving like a pack of wild animals. In less than twenty minutes, but what seemed like hours, moist-nosed Roy Muridae was able to join Wade Snipper on the platform; and the solicitation of pledges and contributions began as the guests, now less agitated, sipped wine and munched on carrots, cauliflower dip and cheese.

Three weeks later, as Dr. Mark Littman walked to his car in the Mid-Atlantic Hospital parking lot, he was startled by thousands of brilliant flashes of red and yellow lights streaking through the clouds and into the stratosphere.

"Holy shit! If the world is coming to an end, why didn't it happen before my eighteen hour shift?", Littman muttered as he scurried from glass and bricks that fell from the hospital's Ellsworth Pavilion. Strangely, the same phenomenon was repeated in thousands of cities and shocked a world long inured to exploding airplanes, jailed religious and political leaders and expensive, inexplicable beer commercials.

The following day in Garfield City, every trap taken to the Patterson Avenue incinerator was empty, and, for the first twenty-four hour period since its inception, the Municipal Rodent Very Hot Line received no calls, except one wrong number from a woman trying to reach the Pro-Choice office.

In suburban Ridgemont, Tommy Bolton searched for two and a half hours but could not find Whispy Chopper, his pet. At Garfield University, researchers found that every cage in the Harrington Chemical, Biological and Psychological Warfare laboratory had been unlocked. Several windows were partially opened, and all the TX-1 albino rats in the building were gone. The somnolent rabbits in Room 303, however, chose to remain.

The reports in Garfield City were, of course, merely anecdotes in a worldwide phenomenon. A number of religious leaders cited references that predicted this happening. Scientists, on the other hand, had no explanation, and newspaper editorials and television commentators suggested that mankind had benefitted from a great miracle. Sadly, once again, mankind has misread the message. (**)

*No rabbits were present to protest the term
**Hopefully, our ability to read messages will improve

HIPPOCRATES AND THE CLASS OF 1987

I swear by Apollo Physician and Asclepius and Hygieia and Panaceia and all the gods and goddesses, making them my witness, that I will fulfill according to my ability and judgment this oath and this covenant:

To hold him who has taught me this art as equal to my parents and to live my life in partnership with him, and if he is in need of money to give him a share of mine,.........

I will neither give a deadly drug to anyone if asked for, nor will make a suggestion to that effect........

I will not give to a woman an abortive remedy.......

I will not use the knife, not even for sufferers of stone.......

> If I fulfill this oath…..may it be granted to me to
> enjoy life and art, being honored with fame……..
> If I transgress it………may the opposite of all this
> be my lot.
>
> Hippocrates
> Prominent Ancient Greek Physician
> *Modified from translation – Michael North, National*
> *Library of Medicine 2002*

"You, my young colleagues, are about to revolutionize medicine," Dr. Lindstrom announced, leaning over the podium in Alumni Hall. "With you leading the way, things will never be the same." They certainly never were.

Despite difficulty reading his notes, having deferred cataract surgery until after the medical revolution, Lindstrom had no doubt that "spectacular advances in the diagnosis and treatment of every disease known to man will defy the imagination." He concluded, to everyone's pleasure, that the future of these young doctors was yet to be realized, or something quite similar.

On that day, June 12, 1987, the graduating class of Mid-Atlantic Medical College, Garfield City, Pennsylvania, recited the Hippocratic Oath, or a facsimile, and received over-sized Doctor of Medicine diplomas. With that, the commencement speaker, Dr. Julian A. Lindstrom, Director-Emeritus of the American Academy of Life-Threatening Illnesses, announced that the graduates, all one hundred and forty two, were entering their chosen profession on the threshold of "The Golden Age of Medicine".

"By the time you reach my age," Lindstrom assured them, "all but the most mundane and stubborn diseases will have been eliminated." He was eighty-four. "People will simply wear out painlessly." The speaker did not touch on how subsequent generations of physicians might spend their time.

Lindstrom could not have guessed that over the next twenty or thirty years, every student, except Bruce Winchester, who became a lawyer, and James Barnett and Lawrence Gilliam, who died, would have violated the oath, some on a daily basis. Quite a few had given deadly drugs, some had given women abortive remedies and four or five had not remained free......"of mischief and, in particular, free of sexual relations with both female and male persons, be they free or slave, in houses they had visited." And regrettably, none "applied dietetic measures for the benefit of the sick," as they had promised.

While, inexplicably, an inordinate number were psychiatrists, nearly fifty of them, despite Hippocrates's recommendation, used the knife and did not "withdraw in favor of such men (i.e. barbers) as are engaged in this work." Most notable in that deviate behavior was Benedict 'Butch' Unger, who, after inadvertently castrating the future president of the United States, must have wished, in fact, that he had withdrawn. Furthermore, there is no evidence that any one in the class of '87 gave money to a needy teacher, and Freddie Highstick, by killing one, unquestionably violated that pledge.

One could argue that the language and content of the Hippocratic Oath is both outdated and quaint; and, despite its inexplicable survival, need not guide the Class of '87 or any other class. In addition, expectations for the achievements of modern scientific medicine, despite Professor Lindstrom's blind faith, may have been unrealistic. Although a few diseases have been eliminated, many new ones have been introduced, some particularly tricky; and it seems unlikely that Lindstrom's prediction will ever come true.

Despite that, there are professional standards; and most patients know what they expect from their physician and from the health care system. While not listed in any statement of ethics, patients do not, for example, expect their doctors to rip out and sell the internal organs of dogs. Hippocrates certainly would have included that in an expanded version. Nor would he, or the modern public, expect physicians to advertise small, shapely noses on TV during half time of football games.

Would old Lindstrom have imagined, as he squinted at the graduates, that one day three of them would be in federal prison, one would be a black-jack dealer (see above), one a realtor, or that many could no longer remember why they had chosen medicine? Or that he himself would die of a routine disease that he had previously scheduled for elimination? If, in fact, the "Golden Age of Medicine" actually came, it must have left while no one was watching.

BIO: JOEL L. CHINITZ M.D., M.P.H.

Joel Chinitz graduated cum laude from The College of Medicine of the State University of New York, Downstate Medical Center in 1962 after election to AOA, the National Medical Honor Society, in 1961. Following military service, residency and fellowship programs, he practiced nephrology in Philadelphia for twenty years and directed the Hahnemann University College of Medicine nephrology curriculum. Dr. Chinitz developed and directed the first out-patient hemodialysis unit in Pennsylvania.

In 1993, in a career change, (*) he completed an MPH program at Temple University while a graduate assistant, and pursued his interest in public health and community medicine. In this second career he was a primary care physician at the Hunting Park Health Center and Medical Director of the Physician Assistant program at Philadelphia University and the Visiting Nurse Association of Greater Philadelphia. Concurrently, he was a volunteer physician at the Kensington Catholic Worker Clinic.

As Community Health Coordinator of Philadelphia Physicians for Social Responsibility (PSR), he developed training programs in domestic violence, bullying prevention and firearm violence for clinicians. He has served on the boards of Philadelphia and National PSR, the Montgomery County Board of Health and Women Against Abuse. He was the 2009 recipient of Philadelphia County Medical Society Practitioner of the Year Award, but his greatest achievements include completing six marathons after age 40 and being tolerated by his wife and three exceptional daughters. Now add grandchildren and sons-in-law to that list. As a recovering Nephrologist, he has given several White Coat Ceremony keynote addresses and most recently has spoken to a range of organizations, academic programs and community groups on the subject "What is Health, How Can I Get Some and How Much Does it Cost?"

*or mid-life crisis

End

Made in the USA
Middletown, DE
15 August 2017